TWELVE MONTHS OF SUNDAYS

Reflections on Bible Readings, Year C

—— ≈ ——

TWELVE MONTHS OF SUNDAYS

Reflections on Bible Readings, Year C

—— ~ ——

N. T. WRIGHT

Published in Great Britain in 2000 by
Society for Promoting Christian Knowledge
Holy Trinity Church
Marylebone Road
London NW1 4DU

British Library Cataloguing-in-Publication Data
A catalogue record for this book
is available from the British Library

ISBN 0–281–05285–9

Typeset by Wilmaset Ltd, Birkenhead, Wirral
Printed in Great Britain by
The Cromwell Press, Trowbridge, Wiltshire

TWELVE MONTHS OF SUNDAYS

N. T. Wright is Canon Theologian of Westminster Abbey, and holds the degree of Doctor of Divinity from Oxford University. He taught New Testament Studies in Cambridge, Montreal and Oxford, and worked as a College Chaplain, before becoming Dean of Lichfield in 1994 and moving to Westminster in 2000. He has written over twenty books about the origins of Christianity and its contemporary relevance, and is currently Chair of the Historical Jesus Section in the Society of Biblical Literature. Dr Wright broadcasts regularly on radio and television. He is married with four young adult children.

Contents

——— ≈ ———

Preface

⎯⎯ ⁓ ⎯⎯

This book brings together my reflections based on the weekly biblical readings in the official lectionary now in use in the Church of England. The pieces first appeared in the *Church Times*; the encouraging response to them suggests that they should be made available in a more permanent form.

The lectionary offers a three-year cycle of readings, set out in *The Christian Year* (Church House Publishing 1997). This first volume of reflections covers Year C, which will come into use in Advent 2000 and every third year thereafter. Two more volumes, covering Years A and B, will follow in succession, completing the set of Sundays in all three years. No attempt has been made to cover the readings for the various Saints' Days that may from time to time fall on a Sunday. Every possible regular Sunday, however, has been covered, including the extra 'Propers' provided after Epiphany when Easter is late and after Trinity when Easter is early. I have used the 'continuous' set of readings for the Sundays in Ordinary Time after Trinity, rather than the 'related' set in each case.

Where the official lectionary suggests a 'passage' consisting of clumps of verses selected out of a longer paragraph or chapter, I have sometimes simply listed, and commented on, the entire passage. I am well aware that it is often impossible to read as much Scripture during the course of a well-ordered liturgy as the integrity of the text might seem to require. But it is important that the serious reader, let alone the preacher, be aware of the whole from which the parts are taken, and interpret those parts in the light of the whole.

I assume that the reader will have the biblical text to hand, preferably in more than one good modern translation. These pieces are not, of course, a full commentary on the passages. They are personal reflections designed to stimulate fresh thought. If they prompt the reader to his or her own exploration, understanding and love of the text, and of the God of whom it speaks, my purpose will have been more than accomplished.

My thanks are due to Paul Handley, Editor of the *Church Times*, and to the editorial assistant Yolande Clarke, for the invitation to write these reflections in the first place and for the patient encouragement which has kept me to the task. I am grateful, too, to SPCK for accepting the project, and to Joanna Moriarty and Mary Matthews who have helped bring it to completion.

N. T. Wright
Epiphany 2000

Advent

The First Sunday of Advent

—— ❧ ——

Jeremiah 33.14–16
1 Thessalonians 3.9–13
Luke 21.25–36

It is January, AD 69. You are a Greek-speaking Christian in a Roman town in Turkey. You are deeply anxious about the fierce war in Judaea: the Romans have laid siege to Jerusalem; the city faces starvation, civil strife and military defeat; many Christians are caught in the middle. Official news from Rome has confirmed that the Emperor, Nero, committed suicide a few months ago, to be succeeded by Galba, a general from the provinces. Now you hear a wild rumour that Galba himself has been killed, that other would-be emperors are staking their claims, and that a major civil war is looming. All the fixed points of your ordinary life are suddenly in question. What language can you borrow to do justice to the reality?

'There will be signs in the sun, the moon, and the stars, and on the earth distress among nations confused by the roaring of the sea and the waves. People will faint from fear of what is coming upon the world, for the powers of the heavens will be shaken.' No, you aren't afraid of sea or sky. You use the language of tidal wave and thunderbolt because nothing else will do. And you continue, drawing on traditions going back to the early Christians who, soaked in Scripture, knew well what such words would mean: 'Then they will see "the Son of Man coming in a cloud" with

2

power and great glory'. No, you don't imagine you will see Jesus flying around in the sky. You know that through these tribulations God will vindicate Jesus, and rescue his people. Up till now, the kingdom Jesus announced had been in tension with the continuing existence of the Jerusalem Temple, whose authorities had sent him to his death. Soon it will be clear which of the two God has vindicated. You cling on to these prophecies and promises for dear life. You have nothing else.

Twenty years pass, and with them the immediate crisis. Jerusalem lies in ruins. Rome has another emperor. You and your fellow Christians have had leisure to reflect on what has, and hasn't, happened. The Church is better established, but the world is still full of wickedness. There must still remain a future fulfilment of God's great, world-changing promises. You continue to tell the story of Jesus' warnings and promises, but the symbols now evoke fresh meanings. God's promise of a new world combines with your longing to be in the royal presence, and under the healing rule, of Jesus himself. Other old sayings, mused on over two generations, give this hope specific focus. 'This Jesus, taken from you into heaven, will come in the same way.' Welcome to Advent: a rich mix of politics, prophecy, prayer and perseverance. Oh, and holiness, too: if the Lord, in his royal presence, will 'establish your hearts unblameable in holiness', it would be as well to live in the present in the mode that is to be vindicated in the future.

The Second Sunday of Advent

———— ∾ ————

Malachi 3.1–4
Philippians 1.3–11
Luke 3.1–6

I must have sung Handel's *Messiah* dozens of times before I asked myself what its first chorus actually meant. 'And the glory of the Lord shall be revealed, and all flesh shall see it together.' It makes what the late Michael Flanders once called 'a jolly pleasing noise'; but what is it about?

In Luke's day, this passage from Isaiah had a well-established place within the wider Jewish longing for restoration. When Solomon built the Temple, 'the glory of Yahweh filled the house'. The 'glory' departed when the Babylonians destroyed the Temple; but, even when the Temple was rebuilt, the glory did not come back. Post-exilic prophets like Malachi saw the return of Yahweh to Zion as still in the future: 'the Lord whom you seek will suddenly come to his Temple'. When that happened, the whole created order would, of course, roll out the red carpet. Valleys would be filled in, mountains flattened, and Yahweh would return in splendour to Jerusalem.

The earliest Christians had the audacity to claim that this had been fulfilled in Jesus. John the Baptist was the voice preparing the way; Jesus was the coming King, the very embodiment of the returning Yahweh. He made his public appearance, as Luke emphasizes, within the imperial worlds of Tiberius Caesar and Herod Antipas. Tiberius styled

4

himself as 'son of the divine Augustus'; with John's ministry, Jesus is revealed as the Son of the one God, Israel's God. Malachi's prophecy of the coming Lord who would purify the priesthood is strangely fulfilled in Jesus' subsequent actions in the Temple courts.

In none of these cases did the reality correspond to what first-century readers of the prophets might have expected. The priesthood remained corrupt. Tiberius and Herod still ruled, and ruled brutally. The Temple had not been filled with the bright cloud of God's presence. Hills and valleys remained intact. Nevertheless, Jesus' life, and supremely his death and resurrection, forced his followers to read the prophecies with new eyes. This, after all, must have been what they were about.

At the same time, a new sense was born, of a fulfilment still to come, completing what had been begun. Paul speaks of the purity promised to God's people as a future reality already breaking in to the present. Jesus has already purified his people, and will bring that process to completion when the Old Testament 'day of the Lord' is translated into New Testament reality. God's people at present are the new nation of priests, summing up the praises, prayers, and pains of creation and presenting them before the redeeming and re-creating God, anticipating the more literal fulfilment of Isaiah's cosmic prophecy, when the whole created order will be set free.

We should not underestimate the cost of the purification necessary for this role. 'He is like a refiner's fire, and like fuller's soap.' I wish Handel had set that whole phrase. I would like to know what he would have done with the soap.

The Third Sunday of Advent

—— ⟳ ——

Zephaniah 3.14–20
Philippians 4.4–7
Luke 3.7–18

The new lectionary has hardly begun, and I fear I am going to grumble about it as I did about its predecessor. How will people ever learn that the Bible and its message are politically relevant – that the proclamation of God's kingdom challenges the kingdoms of the world – if we omit the verses that say so (in this case Luke 3.19–20)?

Josephus tells us that Herod regarded John as a threat. Well, he would, wouldn't he: a fiery prophet drawing crowds and talking about God's kingdom. Luke tells us that John singled out Herod for direct attack. It wasn't just that Herod's marital arrangements were unethical, out of line with God's ideal. The point was that they disqualified Herod from being God's true king. John pointed to Jesus as the genuine king of the Jews; but this meant confronting the claims of the existing king. How could Jesus be the king? Because Herod was a sham. How could you tell that Herod was a sham? Look at his personal life. The attack on Herod, and John's imprisonment and subsequent death, are part of the inner meaning of his kingdom-announcement.

The pattern of polemical kingdom-proclamation is deeply rooted in the Hebrew Scriptures. Zephaniah's message to Israel, of long-awaited joy and relief, needs to include the reassurance that God will deal with all oppressors outside, and all prejudices within, his people. The enemies that have made Israel's life a misery will do so no more; the destructive honour/shame culture that has kept the physically handicapped as second-class citizens will be swept aside. All God's people will join in the great celebration. No one versed in Scriptures such as these could fail to see that they were coming true in the work of Jesus, as the lame and the outcast found themselves healed, welcomed into the family at last.

We can keep the political implications of the gospel at bay by removing some passages; we can achieve the same result by reading others without noticing their wider context. When Paul told the Philippians to 'rejoice in the Lord', he was writing to a Roman colony where 'Lord' meant Caesar, and where celebration was what happened on Caesar's birthday and many similar imperial festivals. Philippi, along with many other cities in Greece and Turkey under Roman rule, relied heavily on the *pax Romana*, the peace which had come after the civil war a century before, and which was maintained by heavy-handed and often brutal rule. Against this ambiguous blessing, Paul places 'the peace of God, which passes all understanding'. In the true King, Jesus, God has won the victory over enemies more dangerous and subtle than those of the Roman state. The Advent hope that God's peace will one day rule in the world enables it now to rule in our hearts, and gives us the courage to proclaim the gospel of the kingdom, even when this means challenging the kingdoms of the world.

The Fourth Sunday of Advent

— ∼ —

Micah 5.2–5a
Hebrews 10.5–10
Luke 1.39–45

'He shall be the one of peace.' We can feel the sigh of relief rising from prophet and hearers alike. To a world of uncertainty, fear, wars and rumours of wars, there comes the news of a king whose rule will establish peace and security. The portrait combines different elements: the child to be born from the house of David, the shepherd who will feed his flock, the peaceful ruler of the entire world, and, more puzzling, one 'whose origin is from of old, from ancient days'. Somehow the coming king will embody the presence, and saving power, of Israel's God.

The letter to the Hebrews evokes a quite different biblical image for the coming of the Messiah into the world, yet it arrives at the same conclusion. The Messiah's coming, the writer declares, fulfils Psalm 40: God's purpose will be accomplished through his utter obedience, which is the reality towards which animal sacrifice points. All that the Temple stood for is thus taken up, rolled together, and focused on the one for whom God has 'prepared a body'. The Messiah's birth, into a life of obedience and vocation, makes even Israel's central symbol redundant. He will be the true meeting place of heaven and earth, the location, concentration and embodiment of God's promise-keeping

8

grace. All the symbols of Israel's life, history and culture point towards the mystery of the incarnation.

It is hard to know how much of this was in Mary's mind or heart as she made her hurried journey to Elizabeth. She was no doubt taken up with the excitement, the shock, the perplexity of finding herself in the situation of which so many Jewish girls down the years had dreamed but which none before her had actually experienced. 'Until the time when she who is in labour has brought forth': Micah's prophecy had but a few months to go. Would she cope? Was she equal to the challenge of such a wonderful and terrible vocation? The great stories of the Bible, with all their large theological and political significance, enhance and do not eliminate the sense of specific persons being caught up within God's drama, finding their own lives turned upside down or perhaps the right way up, being gripped at the heart with God's mysterious presence, feeling the warm breath of his love, discovering a sense of direction to which they have no choice but be obedient. We must, of course, resist the pressure to turn Christmas into a celebration of private feelings and beliefs. That would be to capitulate to our culture's insistence that religion is set apart from Micah's problems, from the pain and politics of the larger world. But, once we recognize in Mary's womb the one 'whose origin is of old, of ancient days', we may find, like Elizabeth, that something leaps within us. The presence in our midst of the Obedient One may become once more the signal, and the means, of fresh vocation, obedience, hope and joy.

Christmas

The First Sunday of Christmas

——— ❧ ———

1 Samuel 2.18–20, 26
Colossians 3.12–17
Luke 2.41–52

The boyhood stories of Jesus and Samuel jar slightly with one another. Samuel's mother deliberately takes him to the Temple in order to leave him there; Jesus' parents intend to take him home, but leave him behind by mistake. Samuel, designated as assistant to Eli, the priest, is then called to be a prophet. Jesus, whom Luke's reader already knows is the appointed King, appears here as a prodigious student of Israel's traditions. For Luke, after all, the closer parallel to Samuel is John the Baptist, not Jesus: John, born by promise to a childless couple, does what Samuel eventually did and anoints the coming King.

Underneath the surface differences runs the same dark theme. Jesus' twelve-year-old visit to the Temple foreshadows his later visit, in Luke 19, where he weeps over the city, pronounces its doom, and goes alone to confront the chief priests once more. Samuel's apprenticing to Eli takes place in the context of increasing evil within Eli's own house; the verses in which this all-too-contemporary corruption is described are omitted by the squeamish lectionary, producing an apparently cosy scene of a happy and devout family where the text offers one of shocking immorality and forebodings of judgement, of which the boy-prophet is to be the herald. (Notice how the same thing happens when

1 Samuel 3 is read out in church, stopping abruptly at verse 10; and, for that matter, Isaiah 6, stopping at verse 8. Clear-cut vocations seem to be associated with unwelcome tasks; hoping for the former without the latter, we muzzle both the text and ourselves.) When Luke, echoing the Samuel story again, says that Jesus increased in wisdom and stature, and in divine and human favour, those with ears to hear will not construe the parallel as indicating a settled, model 'holy family' life, but rather Jesus' strange commissioning and equipping for the task of copying Samuel, bringing God's word of justice to his faithless people.

Luke's story sets up further resonances with his own last chapter. The disciples on the road to Emmaus (husband and wife?) are leaving Jerusalem in sorrow, three days having elapsed after the crashing failure of their dreams. When they rush back to Jerusalem it is with joy, having met the Jesus who had completed his Father's business.

All is not lost, though, for those who still hope that readings about the 'holy family' will offer help for our own somewhat less than holy ones. Paul's bracing injunctions to kindness, gentleness and mutual forgiveness are quite enough to be going on with, simply considered as abstract moral commandments. But they are of course nothing of the kind. They are what happens when the royal life, the Jesus-life, is let loose in persons and communities. The thought of a family, or church, really living out Colossians 3 will puzzle some for whom it appears totally unrealistic. So what? Did they not know that we must be about our Father's business?

The Second Sunday of Christmas

—— ∿ ——

Jeremiah 31.7–14
Ephesians 1.3–14
John 1.1–18

Take a deep breath, and try reading Ephesians 1.3–14 all in one go. It is, after all, a single sentence in the Greek, a Christian version of the Jewish-style prayer, 'Blessed be the God who...'. Only now, instead of the Jewish affirmations, we have a rethought set of Christian ones. God's choice of his special people; their rescue from slavery; his purpose to bless the whole world through them; his offer, and advance guarantee, of an inheritance. Election, exodus, promised land, and the presence of God himself: this is Israel's story, summed up in the Messiah's story and thus made available to those who are 'in him'. Jeremiah's promise of covenant renewal has come true.

This prayer sums up, in form as much as content, the revolution that has occurred within Judaism with the coming of the Messiah. Just as a house-plant may produce inoffensive leaves for years and then suddenly sprout a spectacular flower, so the steady recital of God's mighty acts, looking back many centuries, now gives birth to something which appears novel but which could only have come from within. This prayer belongs firmly in the Jewish tradition, but its focus on one recent individual, its extension of God's promise to a worldwide people, and its latent trinitarianism all proclaim that something new has come to flower with the birth of the Messiah.

Even Ephesians 1 is overshadowed by the opening of John's Gospel. (How on earth can one hope to read these side by side in a church service in such a way as to let their resonances be heard? Answers on a postcard, please.) John 1 is prayer, theology, history, Scripture and (as the advertisements say) much more: a meditation which penetrates quietly into the mystery of God and the world, drawing eye, mind, heart and will into the life and love of the Creator.

Again we find radical innovation at the very centre of Judaism. How does the one transcendent Creator act within, and for the benefit of, his creation? First-century Judaism answers: by his wisdom, his word, his law, his spirit, and his glory (the last of which dwells in the Temple). John 1 offers an extended meditation on Jesus in precisely these categories. The idea that Jesus is 'God incarnate' is not, as often suggested, a move away from Jewish monotheism into speculative Greek philosophy. It is a means of sceing Jesus and the Spirit precisely within Jewish categories. It is the new flower, bursting unexpectedly from the plant.

If this is the God we worship (and if it isn't, then Christmas has indeed been a waste of time) we would do well to ask: what surprising new flowers has he in store for us today? In January 2000, however misleadingly, we celebrated the Millennium. Inside our regular (and often rather tame) celebrations of God's liberation in Jesus, there might be a new flower waiting to be born. Forget the white elephants: what about the Jubilee?

Epiphany

The First Sunday of Epiphany

—— ❧ ——

Isaiah 43.1–7
Acts 8.14–17
Luke 3.15–17, 21–22

We now have the middle of Luke 3 for the second time in four weeks, and verses 19–20 are still missing. This mightn't matter so much if they didn't relate as closely as they do to the underlying themes of the other readings, chosen in this Epiphany season to emphasize the outward movement of the gospel, beyond the confines of Israel, to embrace the rest of the world.

The problem is that the rest of the world doesn't particularly *want* to be embraced, thank you very much, and often takes vigorous steps to prevent any such thing happening. The crowds were wondering if John was the Messiah, the King of the Jews; no, says John, but he is coming. But there already is a king of the Jews, and he doesn't care for rival kingdom-announcements. John's warning of the fire that will burn up the chaff is partly directed at that supreme piece of chaff, Herod Antipas, a shadow no doubt of his malevolent old father, but still capable of brutal overreaction, not least to disturbing prophets. When you celebrate the three kings, remember that not all kings came bearing gifts.

A more subtle confrontation takes place in Samaria. Like a forest fire leaping across a river, the gospel of Jesus has crossed the most obvious racial and cultural barrier, extending from the early Jewish Christians to the despised

18

Samaritans. As a symbolic gesture, the mission of Peter and John was a vital sign of the Epiphany message: Jesus and his Spirit are for all people, not just for the Jews. (That, rather than any theory about apostolic sacramental 'validity', was certainly what Luke saw as the main point of the incident.) But, like all powerful symbolic gestures, this one provoked a reaction, again conveniently omitted in these readings: the local magician tried to make the apostolic gospel part of his arsenal of lucrative trickery, and Peter's and John's mission to Samaria therefore included sharp and necessary rebuke along with glad affirmation.

Behind all such scenes in the New Testament stands the prophetic awareness that the better the news from the true God, the more likely the angry reaction of the false gods (and those who serve them). Isaiah's wonderful message of comfort is based on the character of Israel's God, the powerful healer; but the reason his people are to be encouraged is that the pagan idols that have held them in their grip have been defeated at last. This knowledge alone will enable the prophet's hearers to pass through fire and water without danger. If, ultimately, we have nothing to fear from the loud and threatening gods that range themselves against God's gospel, we have nothing to gain by pretending that their threats, and their temporary power, do not exist. At Epiphany, we do well to recognize that the kingdoms of the world will not always welcome the kingdom of God. The bracing realism of the Bible is the ground of its true comfort.

The Second Sunday of Epiphany

—— ❧ ——

Isaiah 62.1–5
1 Corinthians 12.1–11
John 2.1–11

Nuptial imagery rings through the Bible like a peal of wedding bells. The first two chapters of Genesis reach their climax in the creation of man and woman in God's image; the last two chapters of Revelation unveil the New Jerusalem, dressed as a bride adorned for her husband. In between, weddings form significant steps in the story of God and his people (Isaac/Rebecca, Ruth/Boaz, and many others); marriage failure reflects covenant disaster (Hosea); marriage renewal-after-failure follows the work of the Servant (Isaiah 54). In today's reading, Jerusalem's vindication and glory is to be revealed before the nations, resulting in joy like that of a happy young couple (Isaiah 62). In the New Testament, Ephesians joins Revelation in picturing marriage as a sign and sacrament of Christ's union with his people. The world (or is it just the journalists?) may scorn, sentimentalize or trivialize marriage; God still celebrates it.

Hardly surprising, then, that the first 'sign' of Jesus' glory in John's Gospel takes place at a wedding, and lifts the party to new heights. This 'sign' begins a series; John underlines the second one, too (4.54), and leaves us to work out the rest for ourselves. Though the point is debated, it seems likely that he intends the seventh (or perhaps it's the eighth, the first of a new sequence?) to be the resurrection. The present

20

'sign' takes place 'on the third day', pointing forwards to that great fulfilment. But of course Jesus' glory is fully revealed, as far as John is concerned, on the cross. There, when 'the hour has come' at last, Jesus' strange question (literally 'Woman, what is there to you and me?') is replaced by 'Woman, behold your son; son, behold your mother'. As at Cana Jesus takes the Jewish purification-water and turns it into wine, so at Calvary he takes the Jewish Passover festival and transforms it into the great revelation-in-action of God's glory and love. God has kept the best wine until now: Israel and the world look on in wonder as the true Bridegroom confounds custom and expectation, redeeming Israel and the world in a way neither would have imagined possible.

The only reason for including 1 Corinthians 12 here would have been verse 13, where Paul speaks not only of being immersed in the Spirit, but actually of drinking it. This is reflected in the choice of Psalm 36, where God 'gives his people drink from the river of his delights'. Getting drunk on the Spirit, *à la* Acts 2, is so un-Anglican that the lectionary-mongers seem to have lost their nerve and stopped two verses short. But pause to reflect on God's choice of weddings and wine as signs of glory. When we leave church, or rise from prayer (why does that phrase sound old-fashioned?), would people mistake us for wedding guests? For party-goers? Why not? Did we 'do whatever he tells' us? Did we see his glory and believe?

The Third Sunday of Epiphany

——— ∼ ———

Nehemiah 8.1–3, 5–6, 8–10
1 Corinthians 12.12–31a
Luke 4.14–21

Read the text, and give the sense. Both matter. The first is given, there on the page. The second is risky, a matter of prayer and the Spirit, a deep breath and taking the plunge. History warns of wrong, sometimes dangerous, interpretations. But interpretation is inevitable; not to interpret is still to interpret. History also remembers defining moments when text and interpretation together created a new world. Ezra and his colleagues read the law and explained it, creating not only post-exilic Judaism but, in a measure, today's rabbinic Judaism. Jesus read Isaiah and interpreted it, setting the stage not only for his own career but also, in a measure, for his followers to our own time. What could be more dramatic than reading the law code to a community, defining them as God's people in a new way, causing simultaneous tears and rejoicing? Perhaps only this: reading prophecies which spoke of future blessing, and then declaring that it was already starting to happen.

Ezra's message called forth weeping and celebrating; Jesus' sermon produced both antagonism and loyalty. Luke says that Jesus was already acting 'in the power of the Spirit'; when he applied Isaiah 61 to himself he wasn't simply promoting himself, but explaining what he had been doing. As with other prophecies, being misunderstood came with the package. Ezra had the governor's backing. Jesus stood alone, with Herod not far away, Rome on the horizon, and hostile listeners ready to pounce.

Whatever reception today's expositor may expect, the vocation is the same. Read the text and explain it. Expect it to create and define the community, to evoke joy and sorrow, opposition and enthusiasm. The text may be long forgotten, needing to be dusted down and re-presented. It may be well known, needing to be seen in a new light.

Paul's exposition of the unity of Christ's body provides a case in point. If it were read and expounded before the mutually suspicious churches and Christian groupings of our own day; if it were applied in the power of the Spirit to our bizarre and often anachronistic divisions; should we weep in sorrow at our failure to live by it, or throw our hats in the air at the recognition of our real identity and mutual belonging? If someone declared to us that it was time at last for this Scripture to be fulfilled, would we reject the proposal as dangerous and unworkable, or would we sign up, take the risks, and go with the new movement?

Paul grounds the unity of the Church in the one baptism into Christ's body. If we find it hard to explain the meaning of baptism today, perhaps this is because we are so used to thinking of a variety of different bodies that we can no longer hear what Paul is talking about. Where are today's Ezras, called to read and to teach? Where are today's prophets, prepared to say 'Now is the moment for this to be fulfilled'?

The Fourth Sunday of Epiphany

——— ⁓ ———

Ezekiel 43.27—44.4
1 Corinthians 13.1–13
Luke 2.22–40

Ezekiel had seen the glory of the Lord abandoning Jerusalem and the Temple to their fate (chs 10—11). Fittingly, it is he who describes, in the strange visions of chapters 43—44, the return of that glory. Picking up where Isaiah 40 left off, he points forward to the transcendent and luminous splendour of God's presence in the wondrously restored Temple. In the last line of his book, the name of the new city is *Yahweh shammah*, The Lord is There. Jerusalem's peculiar vocation was to be the place where the God of all the earth would be revealed, lighting up the Temple, the city and ultimately the whole world with his radiant presence.

To get the full flavour of the New Testament's reworkings of this theme, you must imagine a faithful (though often faint and fearful) people living with that promise through generations and even centuries, through false dawns and dashed hopes. Think of pious and learned Jews studying Ezekiel and the other prophets, meditating, praying, waiting and wondering. Think of militant Jews getting fed up sitting around, and opting instead to prepare the way for God's glory by force of arms. And then, after all those years, think of an old man who has nurtured a vision for years, wondering no doubt if it was just a dream, and who one day lifts up his eyes in the Temple, sees a young couple with a baby, and

24

no longer doubts, but knows. And think of an old woman, frail and bent but with bright, deep eyes, who is suddenly found telling everyone that the glory has returned. A light to reveal Israel's God to the Gentiles; glory for Israel herself. It probably wasn't what Ezekiel thought it would look like, but I can see him nodding, slowly and thoughtfully, in the background, and preparing once more to fall on his face in awe and love.

The relevance of 1 Corinthians 13 to this rich theme lies in the fact that 1 Corinthians as a whole portrays the Church, corporately and individually, as the temple of the living God, and that chapter 13 is the letter's artistic and theological climax. The busy, bustling arguments of the earlier chapters, hammering out Christian practice on wisdom, personality cults, sex and marriage, compromise with paganism, and so forth, subside. Rising above them, drawing their many melodies into a majestic chorale, is Paul's poem about love: a love that he can only have learnt from the revelation of God in Jesus, a love that can only be lived by the Spirit of Jesus, a love that is as compelling to contemplate as it is difficult to practise.

The return of God's glory was never to be merely comforting. The fall and rise of many in Israel; a sign to be spoken against; a sword through Mary's soul as well. Dangerous treasure, that, to store up in your heart (Luke 2.51). The same could be said of Paul's message, too.

Ordinary Time

Proper 1

— ∼ —

Isaiah 6.1–13
1 Corinthians 15.1–11
Luke 5.1–11

'The holy seed is its stump.' Isaiah's vision in the Temple leaves him with a dreadful commission, to inform God's people of inevitable exile. The nation will be like a tree felled and burnt. But when the worst has occurred, and the smoke clears away, the stump of the tree, blackened and ugly, may again put forth new shoots. After exile there will be new life. Isaiah's original vision contains a microcosm of the entire book.

Observe how the prophet was prepared for this commission. His vision of the thrice-holy God had filled the house with smoke and his heart with shame. Fear followed swiftly, as the seraph flew to him with a burning coal, surely meaning judgement. And so it did; but that wasn't the end. 'This has touched your lips; your guilt is gone, your sin is covered.' This judgement was cleansing, purifying. So it would be with the nation as a whole. The prophet had to learn in himself the hard truth which he would then announce to the people.

Luke's story of the call of the first disciples has a similar shape, inviting us to remark on the striking new content. Instead of God's glory, shielded by seraphs, filling the house with smoke, we have a young prophet borrowing a boat, teaching the shorebound crowds, and filling Peter's nets with unexpected fish. Peter's response mirrors Isaiah's, recognizing in these events a revelation of Israel's God. But Jesus, like the seraph, does not fulfil Peter's expectations, leaving him to suffer the results of his sin. 'Don't be afraid; from now on you will be catching people alive.' The word for 'catching' in Luke's story is unusual: its metaphorical overtones are not so much of fishing, but of taking prisoners alive as opposed to killing them, hence also of restoring to life someone under the threat of death. Peter is not simply to 'fish for people', but to be God's agent in restoring people to life. Peter, like Isaiah, is to be the mouthpiece of the truth he has just learnt in experience.

Paul puts his own experience of the same strange commissioning into a theological formulation: 'By God's grace I am what I am; and his grace to me was not in vain; but I worked harder than all the rest, yet not I but God's grace that was with me.' The grace that grasped Paul reached out through Paul to grasp others with the good news of God's victory over evil in Jesus' death and resurrection. That, after all, is what we should expect, from Isaiah 6 onwards. At Calvary, the tree is cut down, its stump burnt. On Holy Saturday, the holy seed sleeps in the stump. On Easter morning, a shoot comes forth from the stump, and a branch grows out of the roots. And as God's multi-textured truth thereby takes hold of our hearts and minds, look out: that which God burns into us, we are required to pass on.

Proper 2

—— ∾ ——

Jeremiah 17.5–10
1 Corinthians 15.12–20
Luke 6.17–26

Blessings and woes: the upside-down world of the gospel, addressing, as Jeremiah had done, the heart's self-deceptions, and allowing YHWH to test the mind and search the heart.

The woes read like a list of contemporary media-starring role models. The rich: well, obviously. Those who are filled: if not rich, at least their next meal is assured, probably larger than they actually need. Those who laugh: the careless amusement of those for whom the world is not really a tragedy, merely a joke. Those praised by all: the day I write these words, another Honours List is published, giving welcome recognition to some unsung heroes and heroines, but mostly adding one more trophy to already glittering names.

Woe to them! They are probably false prophets, and will receive their reward. Jesus sounds, not for the last time, like Jeremiah himself. His agenda is designed to shock; nothing less will jolt devious hearts into thinking straight about what really matters. The blessings, equally startling, tell us, again in Jeremiah's language, how to find the stream beside which our roots will stay watered, our leaves green, and our fruit fresh. The poor; those who mourn and weep; those who are hated, reviled, and cast out because of the Son of Man.

30

Blessings on them! We hear the words, but most of us find that our devious heart refuses to take them seriously. Jesus' teaching did not come out of the blue. He did not simply arrive in a town and start talking. He arrived with a previous reputation as a healer; it is historically probable that crowds gathered because of his healings, and stayed to listen to his strange oracles. This teaching was designed not simply to give generalized advice, however extraordinary, about the nature of life in God's kingdom, but to explain the secret of Jesus' power.

A church that deceives itself on such basic matters is likely also to deceive itself when it comes to the resurrection. Paul speaks of the rich/poor divide earlier in the letter. We cannot be sure that it was the rich who doubted the resurrection and the poor who believed it, though some such correlation seems at least plausible. That is how self-deceit often works.

The belief in question – not a general belief in immortality or 'survival', but the specific belief that God will give to all Christ's people a new bodily life corresponding to the transformed body of Jesus' resurrection – puts all present wealth, power and posturing into a totally different light. What passes for contemporary thought about ethics often only asks what it may be allowed to get away with: how far it can go. More self-deception. A genuinely Christian ethic would ask: granted that God is going to create a new world, and give us a newly embodied life, in the future, what sort of life is appropriate in the present? Suddenly Jesus' blessings and woes look remarkably appropriate. Easter unmasks the heart's greatest deceits.

Proper 3

——— ✑ ———

Genesis 45.3–11, 15
1 Corinthians 15.35–38, 42–50
Luke 6.27–38

The resurrection is central to Christianity, not just as a dogma but as a driving principle. Unfortunately, Paul's writing in this, the earliest discussion of it, is dense and difficult, and some of the regular translations don't help.

The key is Paul's contrast between perishable and imperishable. The seed and the plant are not an exact analogy for the old body and the new, but rather a way of demonstrating radical change within basic continuity.

The all-important claim is that 'God gives it a body' (v. 38). It is irrelevant to worry (as did some of the early Fathers) about how God will reassemble the exact atoms and molecules of our present bodies. They are in any case in a constant state of flux, through which matter is shared, not hoarded. Resurrection will be an act of new creation, taking up the old within it, like an architect and builder taking stones from a tumbledown old building and reusing them, enhancing their beauty thereby, within a great cathedral.

The new body, then, will be imperishable, not subject to decay or death. It will be animated, not by the 'soul' that will depart from the present body at death, but by the Spirit; that is the meaning of the 'natural body' and the 'spiritual body' in verse 44. (The common translations 'physical body' and 'spiritual body' give completely the wrong impression, implying a kind of Platonism in which physicality itself is regarded as a second-rate form of existence.)

Thus, when Paul declares (v. 50) that 'flesh and blood cannot inherit the kingdom', he is not suggesting that the resurrection body is what we would call 'non-physical'. As the rest of the passage makes clear, the present physicality, subject to decay and death, has to be transformed. In God's new creation, death is not merely to be redescribed in somewhat more optimistic language (death 'seen as' resurrection, as some have put it), but defeated and reversed. If this were not so, Paul could have answered his initial question ('what sort of body will the resurrected dead possess?') a lot more briefly.

Celebrating God's goodness in redemptive re-creation is the underlying motif of Jesus' charge to love enemies, to be merciful and generous beyond measure, and thereby to reflect the compassionate heart of the heavenly Father. To see all this as a hard challenge, towards which one struggles, is already not only to misunderstand but to disobey. Jesus envisages a life based on God's future, on the lavish and exuberant love of the Creator let loose upon the world once more in healing and grace; he urges us to let the life and love of this God flow through our lives already. We are to be resurrection people, those in whom God's future transforms the present.

That was Joseph's secret. Looking to God's future, he was able to see the present with forgiveness instead of revenge. Instead of the anger we might have expected, we find healing generosity.

The Second Sunday Before Lent

—— ~ ——

Genesis 2.4b–9, 15–25
Revelation 4
Luke 8.22–25

The goodness and the terror of the created world dominate these readings. From the garden in Genesis to the throne-room in Revelation, all that is done reflects God's loving creativity, and his sharing of that creativity with the creatures made in his own image. God's breath in human nostrils is used to give names to the animals, and then finally to lead them in worship. Woven deep into Scripture is the human vocation, to be God's agents in bringing order and joy to the world of rivers and plants, animals and birds, and indeed to one another. Made for relationship with God, with the natural world, and with one another, we know the glory, and the high risk, of our fragile calling.

And then there is the sea: endlessly fascinating, simultaneously sulky and seductive, beckoning and threatening. The American travel writer Paul Theroux expressed bewilderment at English people, in cars or on benches, sitting looking at the sea. Why the puzzle? Like a Wagner opera, operating at levels of symbol and drama which touch the nerves other communications cannot reach, the sea reminds us of forces within and around us that have the potential both for horrible destruction and for spectacular beauty. The sea offers its own daily liturgy of chaos and creation, judgement and salvation; like all good liturgy, it draws us into its rhythm.

Genesis insists that the sea is also God's creature. It is not an alien force, a rival deity. The same is, of course, true of Satan; and the sea, already in the story of Noah God's agent of judgement, steadily becomes, in Jewish thought as elsewhere, the great symbol for the forces of dark malevolence. The Psalms celebrated God's victory over the mighty waters: referring to the Exodus, of course, but with mythological overtones wider than any single event. It was from the sea that the monsters emerged in Daniel 7, to make war on the people of God. In Revelation 4.6, with echoes of Solomon's temple, there is a sea of glass, like crystal, before the throne; chaos and evil still threaten God's plan for his creation, but the promise remains of an Exodus-like redemption (Revelation 15.2). Finally, in the new Jerusalem of Revelation 21, there is no more sea.

Jesus asleep as the sea rages around him: why (so far as I can discover) has no great artist painted that scene? It combines Jesus' serenity in the face of threatening chaos, his sharing the lot of those engulfed by it, and God's rainbow-promise that the mighty waters shall not have the last word. Where is the disciples' faith? Do they not know that Jesus is to be the agent of the new Exodus? Of the kingdom in which Israel's God will rule over the raging sea? As the waves subside, imagination makes contact with long-buried hopes and fears, and memory superimposes psalms and prophecies. Who is this, sovereign over the very symbol of untameable disorder?

The Sunday Next Before Lent

— ∾ —

Exodus 34.29–end
2 Corinthians 3.12—4.2
Luke 9.28–43

The intriguing thing about Moses coming down the mountain with his face shining was that *he didn't know*. He had simply been talking with God; it was only when Aaron and the others met him that he realized, from their reaction, that he had been transformed. He was shining unwittingly with God's glory, and the terrified Israelites requested that he wear a veil.

The story became popular in later Jewish legend, and, with a bizarre misunderstanding, in medieval art: the Hebrew word for 'shining' was mistranslated as 'horned', and several artists painted small horns on Moses' forehead, giving him, to our later eyes, a decidedly sinister appearance. The story in Exodus is itself already somewhat comic, with Moses putting on and taking off his veil by rotation.

In 2 Corinthians 3, Paul seems to assume that Moses wore the veil when speaking the law to the people; he also suggests that the real veil lay, not on Moses' face, but on his hearers' hearts (not 'minds' as in NRSV). His talk about reflecting God's glory is exciting, but the argument is dense and difficult. The key is to realize that Paul is drawing a contrast, not between himself and Moses, but between Moses' hearers and his own. Moses failed to 'get through' because the Israelites' hearts remained hardened against the glorious revelation; but the Spirit of Christ has written God's new covenant on the hearts of believers (3.3–6), giving them 'the light of the knowledge of the glory of God in the face of Jesus Christ' (4.6). As a result, when Paul addresses a group of Christians, he does so with boldness and freedom, because the glory of the gospel, which he is revealing to them, is also shining back at him from his hearers. When they look at one another, they are all gazing, as in a mirror, at the glory of the Lord.

Like Moses, the Corinthians are unaware that they are glory-bearers. They are therefore puzzled, maybe even offended, at Paul's direct and challenging style. Why doesn't he dress up his message with more flowery rhetoric? Answer: when you face a congregation of new covenant people, you can tell it like it is. 'By the open statement of the truth we commend ourselves to everyone's conscience in the sight of God.' Christians must learn to see, by faith, the glory of God shining in one another.

Here, then, is part at least of the meaning of the Transfiguration. This time, the God whom Moses met on the mountain was the incarnate one, on his way to accomplish the new Exodus (Luke 9.31). This time, the glory was to be put into action in challenging the forces of sickness and darkness. This time, the word goes out to all people: 'This is my Son, my Chosen; listen to him.' The hearts, lives and perhaps even the faces of those who hear and obey will be transformed, whether they realize it or not.

Lent

The First Sunday of Lent

———— ∾ ————

Deuteronomy 26.1–11
Romans 10.8b–13
Luke 4.1–13

These readings are not about 'temptation' so much as about true worship. Jesus recognized his temptations as distractions from worshipping and trusting the one true God. To see temptation in terms of rules we would like to break, or impulses we must learn to tame, is to succumb to a second-order temptation: to see temptation itself in terms of negatives.

The truth is very different. Every moment, God calls us to know, love and worship him, and thereby to find and celebrate our genuine humanity, and reflect his image in the world. Temptations lure us to turn away from that privilege and invitation, to lower our gaze, shorten our sights, and settle for second best or worse. The dictionary definition of the Greek word for 'sin' is 'missing the mark'. Sin, like a misfired arrow, drops short of the call to true humanness, to bearing and reflecting God's image.

Jesus maintained a single-minded devotion. His allegiance to his Father overrode immediate bodily desires; it ruled out an easy but costly short cut to his vocation (to be the Lord of the world); it forbade him, by seeking a 'proof' of his status, to challenge the word spoken at his baptism. For him, worshipping the one he knew as Father was larger and richer than all these. The real answer to temptation is not 'God will be cross if I do that', but 'if I do that, I will miss the best that my Father has for me'.

That is why the Israelites, entering the land, were to worship God with their first crops. They could not take the land for granted as an automatic right. Their celebrations were a reminder that it was theirs by God's saving grace alone (Deuteronomy 26.6–9), and a sign, through their hospitality to resident aliens (26.11), that they were channels of grace as well as recipients. Of course, they failed; Jesus' fasting in the wilderness was, among other things, a sign of corporate penitence for a thousand years of rebellion, and a prelude to the establishment of a new people whose sole identifying badge would be neither race, nor territory, but loyalty to God.

Paul indicates that Jesus has indeed become Lord of the whole world, though not by the tempter's route. His faithfulness to his strange vocation of suffering and death is now to be reflected by our faithfulness to him, summed up in our acknowledgement of his universal lordship and our belief in his resurrection from the dead. These striking claims, repeated in our own baptisms, are of course under regular attack. We are thereby regularly tempted, not merely to wrong belief, but to missing out on the best that God has for us, the genuine humanness that Jesus offers to all through the Paschal mystery. As we set out on the wilderness journey of Lent, we do well to reflect on true worship as the ground of true holiness, and true belief as its identifying mark.

The Second Sunday of Lent

—— ～ ——

Genesis 15.1–12, 17–18
Philippians 3.17—4.1
Luke 13.31–end

The question raised by Philippians 3.17 is: how on earth can the Philippian church, Gentile Christians mostly, 'join in imitating' Paul? The chapter so far describes how Paul came to regard his orthodox Jewish background as 'rubbish', and gave it up to gain Christ. What has that to do with them?

Today's epistle urges the Philippians to adopt the same attitude to their own privileges as Paul did to his. They belonged to a Roman colony; and, though Paul could make creative use of his Roman citizenship, his gospel cut across the grain of orthodox Roman belief and practice. Fifty years earlier, the Mediterranean world hailed Augustus as 'saviour' and 'lord'. He had, after all, brought peace (of a sort) to the known world, and ruled unchallenged over an unprecedentedly large empire. Roman citizens, wherever they were, cherished both their status and their security. If enemies threatened, their saviour-lord would come from the mother city to rescue them. By Paul's day, Caesar was openly worshipped, at least in the Eastern Mediterranean.

Verses 20–21 must be read against that background. For the Christian there is only one Saviour and Lord, only one mother city, only one hope. The Philippians must be ready to abandon the imitation in order to embrace the reality. The conclusion of the argument at 4.1 (congratulations to the lectionary for getting it right), encourages them to find their identity and security in this 'Lord' and in nobody else.

They are, in consequence, to engage in the same holy boldness with which Jesus, at one remove, confronted Herod. Herod may only have been a tinpot little monarch compared with Caesar, but his sly threats were real enough. Jesus had sovereign confidence in God's overarching plan: when he declares it impossible for a prophet to die outside Jerusalem, he is not making a statement about history so much as asserting that his own prophetic vocation, which his divine commissioner would safeguard, would be accomplished there and there only. He would be enthroned, however paradoxically, in Jerusalem, and Herod would be shown up as the impostor. The way of the cross, trodden by Jesus and commended by Paul, undercuts the claims of the rulers of this world.

It thereby also fulfils the ancient promise to Abram. At the start of Genesis 15, Abram doesn't even have an heir; by the end, he has been promised both an innumerable family and a substantial territory. The former will gain the latter through the hard road of slavery and rescue, the Old Testament's way of the cross (vv. 13–16). And, as Paul encourages the Philippians to lift their eyes to the heavenly Jerusalem, so God tells Abram to look to the starry heavens to see the wide extent of his promise. No good keeping one's eyes on the present rulers of Egypt or Canaan, of Galilee or Rome; God's kingdom will come on earth as in heaven, and it will come by the way of the cross.

The Third Sunday of Lent

—— ∼ ——

Isaiah 55.1–9
1 Corinthians 10.1–13
Luke 13.1–9

Just in case anyone thought the Old Testament was all gloomy and the New cheerful, here are two passages of dire warning from the New Testament preceded by a warm, redeeming invitation from the Old. Underlying both is God's summons to accept his mercy and his way now, while there is time: 'Seek the Lord while he may be found, call on him while he is near.' Unstated, but powerfully implied, is the message which Isaiah has in common with Luke's Jesus. 'The time may come when you will wish you had.'

Jesus' warnings about coming judgement should not be mistaken for old-fashioned hell-fire preaching. Focus on the 'likewise' in verses 3 and 5: 'Unless you repent, you will perish as they did.' Who are 'they'? The Galileans cut down by Roman swords in the Temple; the Jerusalemites crushed when the tower of Siloam fell. What does 'repent' mean in this context, then? Not simply 'give up your private sins'; rather, 'turn from your headlong flight away from God's mercy, from your quest for your own national salvation by rebellion against Rome.' Unless you give it up, Roman swords and falling stonework will be your lot, not as an arbitrary punishment from a vengeful God but as the direct result of the way you have freely chosen, following your own thoughts rather than God's thoughts. Jesus' tough little

44

parable, then, relates directly to his own work: he has been coming to Israel, seeking fruit and finding none, and now is offering one last chance. As he says at the end of the chapter, he has longed to gather Jerusalem as a hen gathers her chicks for safety under her wings, but the offer has been refused.

Worryingly, Paul confronts Christians with more or less the same challenge. Don't think that baptism and eucharist will magically save you; they put you in the same position as the Israelites in the wilderness, and look what happened to them. Gospel symbols invoke God's presence, but doing that while misbehaving is thumbing one's nose at divine mercy. 1 Corinthians 10 joins strong sacramental and pastoral theology. When faced with idolatry or immorality, Paul doesn't pretend that baptism and eucharist don't mean anything, but nor does he suggest that they exempt one from moral obligation. Nor, however, does he suppose that Christians have to meet this challenge unaided. Amid stormy temptations, they are to cling to the faithfulness of God, who will enable them to come through.

Back, then, to Isaiah. Why does he explain the invitation to return (vv. 6–7) by saying that God thinks differently from how we do (vv. 8–9)? Presumably because no human being would have been faithful and merciful when faced with Israel's rebellion. Isaiah appeals to the transcendence of God, not to frighten, but to explain just how much more generous and merciful God is than we could ever have imagined. Not for nothing is he called, in the old sense, the evangelical prophet.

The Fourth Sunday of Lent

—— ∾ ——

Joshua 5.9–12
2 Corinthians 5.16–end
Luke 15.1–3, 11b–end

At Gilgal the Israelites, like the prodigal, exchanged the food of the wilderness for the food of home. In a dense little scene, explicable only in its wider context, the covenant signs come rushing together: Jordan, circumcision, passover, the fruit of the land. From that moment on, without as yet a sword drawn or a city taken, the Israelites had come home.

Come home, moreover, without reproach. Scholars seem uncertain what 'the disgrace of Egypt' means, or why having the nation circumcised would roll it away. It can't mean that Israel had been in an 'Egyptian', i.e. uncircumcised, condition: the Egyptians were themselves circumcised. More likely, perhaps, that the Egyptians would have despised Israel: yes, they've escaped, but they are only dirty, uncircumcised people, so it doesn't matter. From Gilgal onwards, this taunt is removed. Israel is God's free covenant people, without reproach. No more manna, no more uncircumcision, no more wilderness: the old has passed away, all is become new, as Paul puts it in his spectacular discussion of the ministry of reconciliation.

We are inclined to get carried away in a passage like this, and to forget what it's really all about. It is an explanation of Paul's apostolic ministry. Paul stands on the promised-land side of the Jordan, refusing to look at anyone from the

46

perspective of the 'flesh', the previous wilderness existence. What matters is Christ, and the new creation in him; because of God's action, reconciliation between Creator and creation is now a fact of history, and must be implemented. That is the thrust of the last two verses of chapter 5. Paul does not say 'we entreat *you* on behalf of Christ', but just 'we entreat'; he is describing his ministry, not appealing to the Corinthians. And 'the righteousness of God' in 5.21 is not the status of the justified sinner, but God's covenant faithfulness, which the apostles embody as well as announce. They are to be themselves people who inhabit the further side of the Jordan, living evidence that God has rolled away the reproach of his creation. They thus invite others to join them.

Reconciliation in New Testament terms means the Prodigal Son, one of the few remaining passages which almost everyone in the congregation will already know, or think they know. The story is its own meaning; no summary, no painting even, can replace it. Yet its very familiarity is a challenge: how can we bring it to life once more, prevent the sense of *déjà vu*? Try thinking it through with the Exodus symbolism fresh in mind: the young son in the wilderness, eating desert food until he comes home to the fatted calf; the father ready to roll away all reproach. But this time the reproach comes, not from outsiders, but from within. How can this reconciliation be other than scandalous? And, as at Gilgal, a strange sense of something gained and much still to achieve. What did the Prodigal Son do the next morning?

The Fifth Sunday of Lent
(Passiontide begins)

—— ∾ ——

Isaiah 43.16–21
Philippians 3.4b–14
John 12.1–8

Two stark characterizations from John: the full-blown devotion of Mary and the brooding cynicism of Judas. (On Mondays, Wednesdays and Fridays I think this may perhaps be the same story as that in Luke 7, where the woman is a 'sinner' and the host, and chief grumbler, is a Pharisee called Simon. Writing this on a Thursday, I acknowledge that the host in Matthew's and Mark's parallel to John is called Simon, but I still think Luke is talking about a different occasion.) Lazarus is alive again, and his sisters play out their accustomed roles, Martha serving and Mary at Jesus' feet. Modern cities fill with noise, ancient ones (in the pre-soap days) with smell; Mary's perfume wafts its welcome fragrance all through the house. Of course it's outrageous, over the top. That's the point. Brothers don't get raised from the dead every day.

But whenever people worship Jesus with everything they've got, there's always someone in the background muttering that there's no such thing as a free jar of ointment. We watch in horror at the disintegration of Judas. First, we assume, his devotion has evaporated then his loyalty, then his honesty towards others (his thieving), then his honesty towards himself (as in the present passage, where he says one thing, no doubt telling himself he really means it, while in fact meaning another), then, not long afterwards, his ability to choose good over evil altogether. The downward slope starts gently, but gets steeper. Judas goes on choosing a world which revolves around himself, which then itself deconstructs. Judas symbolizes the way of self-destruction, just as Mary stands for the way of self-giving. Both are costly, but in utterly different ways: 'consumed by either fire or fire'.

Paul went through the process twice over. First, he gave up everything – his pride of birth, upbringing and character – in order to obey the crazy gospel of the crucified Messiah. Then, he discovered that following this Messiah meant a continual self-giving, pouring out his own energy, devotion and life itself at the feet of the one who had 'made him his own'. Jesus validated Mary's devotion by referring to his own approaching death; that same death was woven so deeply into the fabric of Paul's thinking that his life was now dedicated, as he says elsewhere, to filling the world with the fragrance of the gospel.

The contrast of Mary and Judas, the one surprising by depth of devotion, the other by depth of deceit, runs back through Scripture, as would have been plain had the reading from Isaiah gone on another couple of verses. The creator and redeemer God makes rivers flow in the desert, and paths appear in the sea. The wild animals look on and pay him homage. Israel, the people for whose benefit these mighty acts are done, looks the other way, bored and sulky. Worth taking a minute, at this stage of Lent, to reflect on what smell we're giving off.

Palm Sunday
(Liturgy of the Passion)

—— ∽ ——

Isaiah 50.4–9a
Philippians 2.5–11
Luke 22.14—23.56

Isaiah 50 strikes a jarring note in the Palm Sunday celebrations. Which is just as well: we know the end of the story, the fickleness of the crowd, the turning of cheers to jeers. The only Hosannas that count are those that come afterwards, anticipating the day when every knee shall bow. Much as I enjoy Palm Sunday, I can't help remembering that, when he was riding the donkey, Jesus was in tears.

The controlling theme here is *obedience*. The strange plan of salvation is delegated to one who will hear and obey, hear and pass the message on, hear and remain loyal in listening, speaking and above all suffering. We find it hard, almost impossible, to think of God allowing, let alone requiring, suffering from his obedient chosen one(s). We react angrily to Abraham's call to sacrifice Isaac (even though it was rescinded). A colleague in a recent conference spoke of some atonement-theologies as implicating God in 'cosmic child-abuse'.

Yet the sufferings of the Servant remain haunting and evocative, part of the richest tellings of the deepest stories. They resonate with our deep sense that our world is out of joint (strange, isn't it, that those who grumble if you say

50

there's something deeply wrong with the world, on the grounds that that's negative and pessimistic, are the same ones who also grumble if you say that Jesus has saved the world, on the grounds that it's still such a mess). Redemption, if it's to happen at all, must deal with the depth of the pain.

Equally, these stories resonate with our sense, nurtured through meditating (as today) on the passion of Jesus himself, that if there is a redeeming God he must be like this: not solving the problem at arm's length, delegating it down the line, looking on impassively as someone else sorts out the mess, but strangely present, bearing the load in person, acting out the job description which had been offered to Israel, God's servant, but which Israel was incapable of fulfilling.

Pour all that meditation into a mind at once analytic and poetic, stir vigorously, and allow to settle. Result? Philippians 2.5–11: a dense, detailed, pithy vignette of Jesus as the obedient servant, now exalted (as the Messiah was to be) as Lord of the world. It is more, too: a striking, indeed stunning vignette of the God who is revealed precisely *as* the obedient servant, the God who wept on the donkey, remained obedient in Gethsemane, accepted total humiliation and death, and who thus came to the lowest point of human experience, the place where the world's pain seemed to be concentrated, that he might take it upon himself and so exhaust it. If you want to know why we believe in the Trinity, forget the Greek metaphysics, clear your mind of those muddled Hosannas, and live through Holy Week with Paul in your head, the gospel story before your eyes, and hushed wonder in your heart.

Easter

Easter Day

___ ~ ___

Isaiah 65.17–25
1 Corinthians 15.19–26
Luke 24.1–12

'It seemed to them an idle tale.' In Jesus' world, nobody thought of 'resurrection' as happening to one person within ongoing history. It would happen at the very end, when God would raise all his people to share in the new heavens and new earth of prophetic promise. Nothing there about a dead-and-buried person being transformed or re-embodied.

This makes it hard to imagine that the Easter stories resulted from wishful thinking, or from what is sometimes called 'cognitive dissonance', in which people restate their hopes rather than face disappointment. Plenty of people in first-century Judaism had hopes (nationalistic, messianic, libertarian) dashed again and again. None of them went around saying that the dream had in fact come true, though not in the way they had expected. Except the Christians.

What they did say was not what you might have expected. An empty tomb; a rumour of angels; disbelief and puzzlement. No heroics, no great faith, no instant sense of everything clicking into place. Rather, a new tune, starting so quietly that by the time you hear it it's already well under way, growing and swelling into music so rich, so powerful as to make you want to dance and cry at the same time. The resurrection *had already happened*, had come forward to meet them, God's future rushing like an express train into the present, into the middle of history, the middle of the world's pain, of Israel's broken kingdom-dreams. The kingdom had arrived in an unready world, like grand guests stepping out of the Rolls-Royce to find the family having breakfast in pyjamas.

The women rushing around in the early morning, Peter scratching his head staring at empty grave-clothes, might well be puzzled: this was not part of the plan. They had thought Jesus' language about his own dying, and rising again, to be a dark metaphor, indicating perhaps a great struggle against paganism or Israel's current leaders, followed by a great victory. They had not reckoned with it being literal, or with the battle being waged against the last enemy, death itself. They were going to have to get used to living in a present which was shot through with God's future, a world in which the continuing disjointedness of creation was to be seen as out of date, waiting to be brought into line with the future which had already begun to happen.

Paul wrestles with the implications of an 'end' that has already happened and an 'end' which is yet to happen, but he did not invent the idea. It came with the message of the first Easter morning. The world was now to be seen, neither as a tired old system going round and round without hope or meaning, nor as a sick joke in which intimations of immortality always ran into the brick wall of death and cynicism, but in terms of new grass and spring flowers growing through a fresh crack in a concrete slab.

The Second Sunday of Easter

—— ❧ ——

Acts 5.27–32
Revelation 1.4–8
John 20.19–end

The report of Jesus' resurrection strikes the chief priests as a threat of God's judgement. Yes and no, reply the apostles: your guilt is swallowed up in the message of forgiveness, of new Spirit-given life. But those whose way of life seems threatened by the gospel will always interpret it as bad news. Authorities regularly try to suppress or marginalize the gospel, rightly interpreting it as a challenge to their precarious position. But the resurrection is not another human scheme, one power-play alongside others. It is on a different level, God's gift to his surprised world.

It does, of course, challenge rulers who suppose themselves to be utterly supreme, answerable to nobody but themselves. This is the constant message of the book of Revelation: Jesus is the faithful witness, the first-born of the dead, the ruler of kings of the earth. One day his kingship will be universally acknowledged; for the moment, the resurrection has inaugurated him as king-in-waiting, already enthroned but yet to establish his rule visibly and publicly.

Christianity, then, did not begin as, nor is it best characterized in terms of, a pattern of spirituality (a particular way of sensing the presence of God), a code of ethics (a particular variation on the codes which are, broadly speaking, common to most religions), or even a set of doctrines. Of course, it invites people to experience God's presence, to know his will, and to believe his truth; indeed, if understood correctly, it must include all three. But it begins as a challenge to *allegiance*. There cannot be two kings of kings and lords of lords.

In the world addressed by Revelation, there was already a claimant for that title, enthroned in Rome, ruling an empire acquired and maintained by brute force. John's vision is of a different king, ruling a different empire, having gained his dominion by suffering and maintaining it by forgiveness. No wonder other priests and kings tremble at the thought. No power on earth can stand before total, divine, self-giving love.

What is more, this power is *shared*. 'He has made *us* kings and priests, serving God.' Jesus is to be imitated, and his mission implemented, by his Spirit-filled followers: 'As the Father has sent me, so I send you.' As – so: to stand before priests and rulers, to proclaim God's kingdom established through the saving lordship of Jesus, to announce the forgiveness, or the retention, of sins. Not to entice souls into private piety or otherworldly salvation, but to confront the powers of the world with the loving, life-giving power of God.

Maybe it was this challenge, implicit in Jesus' resurrection, that kept Thomas from believing. Scepticism often conceals an element of self-preservation. Belief is not mere mental assent; it is life-changing. And the life into which it changes you comes with a royal and priestly commission attached. When Jesus said 'Peace be with you', he wasn't assuring his followers of a quiet life.

The Third Sunday of Easter

—— ᴄᴠ ——

Acts 9.1–20
Revelation 5.11–14
John 21.1–19

John 21 contains in microcosmic form most of the elements of the previous narrative. We are back in Galilee, with Peter and his friends going fishing. Jesus reveals himself as he had done throughout. He feeds them by the lake. He offers forgiveness, challenge and commission.

Only now, instead of the drama moving forward inexorably to Calvary and Easter, it moves out from there. The fishing, the feeding, the forgiveness and the challenge are all shot through with a sense of something accomplished now to be worked out, something achieved that must now be implemented, something which Jesus has done which must now sweep Peter and the rest along in the tidal wave of new life, new possibilities. The scene is full of a sense of freshness and wonder: sunrise, lake and breakfast picnic hint at the transformation of creation itself.

The whole story is pervaded with this sense of transformation. 'None of the disciples dared ask him, "Who are you?", because they knew it was the Lord.' Jesus is the same, yet somehow different. He is described as a man among men, yet he has somehow been changed. The resurrection is a thoroughly Jewish belief, yet nothing in Judaism had prepared the disciples for this.

The transformation spreads through the scene. Fishing,

after a night of hard and fruitless work, becomes a sudden morning surprise. The conversation Peter needed but no doubt dreaded transformed his denials into stumbling affirmations of love and loyalty, with Jesus' questions themselves being turned into commissions: feed my lambs, tend my sheep, feed my sheep. Finally, the transformation of vocation itself: no longer is Peter to be Jesus' blustering right-hand man, ready (so he thought) to die for Jesus (13.37) out of a sense of pride and self-importance; rather, because Jesus has laid down his life for Peter, Peter will in turn glorify God by his own humbling martyrdom. What more natural, what more utterly challenging, than the simple command, 'Follow me'?

Everything is different in the light of Easter, even God. 'To him who sits on the throne, and to the Lamb, be blessing and honour and glory and might.' Jewish monotheistic worship has been transformed from within, so that the one God is now known in terms of the Lamb and his victory. And what John gives us in narrative form, the author of Revelation gives us in poetry: creation at every level now celebrates that victory and its results.

Revelation 4 and 5 are not, of course, a vision of the future. They portray the throne-room within which visions of the future will be shown to the writer, but they themselves offer a glimpse of what is going on, night and day, in the present time. The question that has faced the world since Easter is the question that confronted Paul on the road to Damascus: granted that a new, transforming reality is let loose in the world, are we prepared to join in the song?

The Fourth Sunday of Easter

—— ∼ ——

Acts 9.36–43
Revelation 7.9–17
John 10.22–30

Within the Easter kaleidoscope, the Lamb becomes the Shepherd. John 10 is already complex enough, with Jesus as both 'shepherd' and 'door', but Revelation characteristically twists the imagery round once more, and the shepherd himself turns out to be the lamb that was slain. Thus is confirmed the radical redefinition of leadership in God's economy: a meek, unwilling prophet in Exodus, a little child in Isaiah, and now a slaughtered lamb.

Jesus' shepherd-discourse takes place at Hanukkah, the feast of the Dedication, commemorating the victory of Judas Maccabeus over the Syrians, his cleansing and rededication of the Temple, and his consequent founding of a hundred-year royal house. With 'shepherd' a regular biblical image for 'king', anyone talking about themselves as the true shepherd, not least at that festival, must have been offering themselves, however cryptically, as God's anointed. But what Jesus says about the shepherd's role and task is so unlike the warlike Maccabean pattern that it becomes almost incomprehensible. Kingdoms without justice, said Augustine, are simply regimes of brigands. Jesus goes further: kingdoms based on anything less than self-giving love are brigandish distortions of the real thing.

Jesus' 'sheep' are therefore those who hear and receive his

60

message of a different kingdom. His life-work has revealed God at work climactically in and through him, and many have accepted his redefinition of kingship; but many do not, because they are hell-bent on a vision of the 'age to come' which will be attained through the establishment of a worldly kingdom.

We are perhaps too eager to translate the Johannine phrase 'eternal life' into something less Jewish, more Platonic, suggesting simply an endless state of disembodied post-mortem bliss. In the first-century Jewish world, the phrase meant primarily 'the life of the coming age', the new age in which wrongs would be righted, sins forgiven and God would be all in all. That is what Jesus was claiming to offer. And he was claiming that, despite the pressure among his contemporaries to seek a Maccabean-style solution to their present plight, God had ensured that some at least would follow him and find thereby the narrow way that would lead to life. In this, as in all things, Jesus and the Father were hand in glove.

It remains a mystery why one or two deaths in the early Church were perceived as intruders to be repelled, at least for the moment, while most, presumably, were mourned but accepted. Peter's raising of Dorcas stands out, fitting into the story as part of the preamble to his visit, immediately afterwards, to Cornelius, the first (or at least the first high-profile) Gentile convert. The message of new life, dramatically acted out in sharp focus from time to time, was part of the strange means by which the Good Shepherd called other sheep to join the great multitude that no one can number, those who trust him to wipe away every tear from their eyes.

The Fifth Sunday of Easter

——— ❧ ———

Acts 11.1–18
Revelation 21.1–6
John 13.31–35

You only discover the flavour of today's Gospel if you remember that it comes immediately after Judas's departure, and immediately before Peter's rash promise to lay down his life for Jesus – and Jesus' sorrowful prediction of Peter's triple denial. Like a warm fire glowing all the brighter as the wind starts to howl and the snow to fall, Jesus' parting promise and commandment sparkle out against the dark backcloth of betrayal and disloyalty.

The promise is characteristically Johannine. Now at last God will be truly glorified. Somehow, what will happen to Jesus will both reveal and exalt the God of Israel, the one Jesus called 'father'; this will show God, so to speak, in his true colours, will unveil the divine love in all its glory. As John puts it at the start of the chapter, Jesus knew that he had come from God and was going to God, and so, having loved his own, he loved them to the uttermost. What he did on the cross was the true and complete expression of what it meant to be precisely the one who had come from God and was going back.

The command which follows is therefore anything but arbitrary. It isn't that Jesus had a particular thing about people loving each other, his own idiosyncratic addition to an ever-increasing store of miscellaneous ethical maxims. It

62

is, rather, that just as his own life, and approaching death, were the true expression of the Father's heart, so he intends his followers to become a further, and continuing, re-embodiment of that same love. This would, of course, be unthinkable without the gift of the Spirit; hardly surprisingly, that is precisely what is promised in the rest of the discourse. The fire which Jesus has lit in the cold, dark night is to be the first in a line of beacons, stretching away into the future and out into the rest of the world, true evidences of the true God, and of the accomplishment of Jesus.

Acts highlights Peter's visit to Cornelius as one key moment in that story. Here, 'love' is not so much a feeling that binds Peter and the new Gentile converts, but the act of obedience in which Peter recognizes Cornelius and his household as his brothers and sisters in Christ, without respect of race. Another beacon: the Spirit told Peter to go somewhere he'd never have dreamed of going; the Spirit fell on Peter's hearers in the first minute or so of his discourse. And, though the Spirit is not mentioned in Revelation at the moment when the new Jerusalem comes down as a bride adorned for her husband, the uniting of God and his people, and his tender healing of all their hurts, are themselves the ultimate end of the story, the victory of love over all that distorts and defaces, damages and destroys, God's good and beautiful world. Why, in the unwisdom of the lectionary, did we have to stop at verse 6?

The Sixth Sunday of Easter

— ∽ —

Acts 16.9–15
Revelation 21.10, 22—22.5
John 14.23–29

No Temple, no sun or moon, and no uncleanness either. A world without evil is, to us, as inconceivable as a world without sun and moon – or, for first-century Jews, a holy city without a Temple. In the new creation, reality will be transformed so that wickedness is as impossible as sun, moon and Temple are unnecessary.

As in John's farewell discourses, the clue is the mysterious personal presence of God himself. Thus, Moses' greatest spiritual battle was not his tussle with Pharaoh and the magicians of Egypt, but with God on Sinai in Exodus 32—34.

Moses managed to persuade God – almost, one might say, against God's better judgement – that his own presence, not merely his angel, would go with Israel to the promised land, despite Israel's rebellion and idolatry. The wilderness tabernacle became a sign of this presence, making Moses' face shine when he went in; and it was eventually institutionalized in the Temple, with all the attendant dangers of presumption, of taking God for granted. Now, in the new creation, symbols give way to reality: God himself will be personally present, and the whole city will shine with his light.

This city will truly be that for which Israel longed through

64

her years of groaning exile. Imagery from Isaiah, Micah, Zechariah and, above all, Ezekiel swirls around here, though in each case transcended: to this city the nations will bring their treasures, and from it healing and blessing will flow out to the world.

The city is not, then, the totality of God's eventual new world; it is the focal point of a world which will finally see God's light and discover his healing. The river of life-giving water, like the rivers of Eden, will flow from it, fulfilling Ezekiel's vision of a river making even the Dead Sea fresh. Worship and mission will still be realities in God's new world. But worship will be face to face, not through a glass darkly; and mission will meet no resistance, as God's healing embraces all creation.

Images of the future are vital to beckon us along the way. But they do more: they work backwards, as it were, towards us, shedding light on our present darkness. Jesus promises a peace which nothing in the present world can provide, a peace which comes from, and points to, God's future.

This is what happens when God himself, Father, Son and Spirit, comes to be at home with, and even in, those who love God and keep his word, anticipating in the present the promise of the new holy city.

On the ground, this reality regularly breaks into our plans and possibilities. Paul, frustrated at being unable to move ahead with work in Asia, is unexpectedly called across to the leading cities of Europe, and finds hearts and minds ready and waiting for the gospel. He and his colleagues, going to stay at Lydia's home, embody in themselves the promise of God's personal presence with his renewed people.

The Seventh Sunday of Easter
(Sunday after Ascension Day)

——— ∼ ———

Acts 16.16–34
Revelation 22.12–14, 16–17, 20–21
John 17.20–end

If Luke had wanted to play down the trouble caused by the gospel, he would quietly have omitted the Philippi story. Healing for one person means loss of money for others, and produces political and cultural charges which, though a blatant cover for self-interest, have sufficient plausibility to result in beatings and imprisonment.

They are Jews, said the angry slave-owners. Yes, but most other Jews lived alongside Gentiles without trouble. The real problem was that Paul and Silas were teaching and representing a way of life in which Roman customs, particularly allegiance to Caesar, were not the guiding rule. As in Thessalonica, they believed in a different king, a different empire. When the gospel landed in Europe, the first thing the authorities said was 'Treason!'.

The story of the earthquake and the jailer can thus be read on at least two levels. Wherever Paul went, there were earthquakes: the Roman world, and communities and individuals within it, were turned upside down by the power of Jesus' name. A pity we miss the last paragraph, in which Paul, despite having upended their world, reminds the magistrates of their duty. This twist completes the delicate and ironic balance of church–state relations in the nascent European Church.

Omitting a paragraph because of length is one thing. Snipping out three verses because they warn that some styles of behaviour have no place in God's holy city is something else. Or do we want to avoid the scandal of the gospel, not only in the world but also in the Church? It is particularly galling to omit 22.19: cutting out the verse that tells you not to cut out verses is the ultimate in Bible-reading *chutzpah*.

Don't let this prissiness distract from the picture of Jesus which these warnings surround: there is enough imagery here for a hall of mirrors, and that may be the point. The glittering and dazzling portrayal of Jesus, the Alpha and Omega, the bright morning star, is meant to lead the eye away from all other distractions and allegiances. By contemplating this Jesus we fulfil his own prayer: that we may be with him where he is, to see his glory, begotten of the Father's love. The vision of God's glory, denied to Moses, is granted in Jesus Christ.

The central characteristic of that vision is of course love: God's love for Jesus and, through Jesus, for all his people; the love of God's people for one another, creating a unity which will indeed reveal to the world the disturbing message that there is another way of being human. Disunity may perhaps be the ultimate worldliness, since it means accepting that we are defined, in the last analysis, by something other than the love of God in Jesus Christ. Let the midnight feast in the jailer's house stand for the joyful meal which will occur when all Christians realize that they belong at the same table. Now that really would be an earthquake.

Day of Pentecost

—— ✌ ——

Acts 2.1–21
Romans 8.14–17
John 14.8–17

The Israelites had been aware of certain persons in their midst, unpredictable and untameable, in whom the Spirit of YHWH dwelt. They spoke his word, led his people, encouraged, rebuked, prayed for and agonized over Israel. They were a sign of God's care and love for his wayward people. But several prophets recognized that this state of affairs could not be God's final will for his people. Jeremiah declared that all God's people would know him, from the least to the greatest. Isaiah threw open the blessings of the Davidic covenant to all who would seek the Lord. And Joel, quoted by Peter at Pentecost, declared that the Spirit of YHWH would be poured out upon people of all sorts. No longer a special élite: young and old, male and female, slave and free alike, all would be caught up by the rushing wind of the prophetic Spirit.

The first disciples were therefore as much struck by the implications of the sudden outpouring of the Spirit as by the manifestations. It wasn't the excitement of being heard speaking in a dozen different languages, dramatic though that was (and is, when it happens today); it was the fact that the Spirit was thereby showing that the long-prophesied coming day had arrived. With the death and resurrection of Jesus, the new age had dawned, and the outpoured Spirit was the confirmation. The point of Pentecost was not so much the offer of a new spiritual experience as the declaration of a new spiritual reality. God's history with the world had turned its decisive corner.

Grasped by this vision, the early Christians went back again and again to the greatest of Jewish stories, the Exodus. Paul deliberately uses Exodus-language to describe where Christians are in God's story – and at the same time to lay to rest any suggestion that because we are living in God's new day there's nothing more to work at (or the counter-suggestion that, because the world is still in a mess, Pentecost can't really have meant a new start for the world). The Church is now in the position of the Israelites in the wilderness: led by God's Spirit, assured of adoption as God's children, walking resolutely away from slavery and towards their inheritance, suffering in the present but confident of the future. And the 'inheritance', as Paul indicates in Romans 4.13 and 8.18–25, is not a single promised land but the whole redeemed creation.

The intimacy and ecstasy of the Spirit's personal in-dwelling, and the fact that with this the world has turned a new corner, lead to those clear, simple profundities which otherwise appear opaque and complex. 'Whatever you ask for will be granted.' 'Keep my commandments.' The Spirit of truth, still incomprehensible to the world, will be with you and in you, so that you may be sent into the world as re-embodiments of the incarnate Son, a sign of God's care and love for his wayward world.

Ordinary Time

Trinity Sunday

——— ⟨∿⟩ ———

Proverbs 8.1–4, 22–31
Romans 5.1–5
John 16.12–15

Deep inside classic Jewish monotheism there lies a strange, swirling sense of a rhythm of mutual relations within the very being of the one God: a to-and-fro, a give-and-take, a command-and-obey, a sense of love poured out and love received. God's Spirit broods over the waters, God's Word goes forth to produce new life, God's Law guides his people, God's Presence or Glory dwells with them in fiery cloud, in tabernacle and temple. These four ways of speaking move to and fro from metaphor to trembling reality-claim and back again. They enable people to speak simultaneously of God's sovereign supremacy and his intimate presence, of his unapproachable holiness and his self-giving love.

The best known is perhaps the fifth. God's Wisdom is his handmaid in creation, the first-born of his works, his chief of staff, his delight. Through the Lady Wisdom of Proverbs 1—8 (contrasting sharply with Mistress Folly, her parody, and her rival for human affection) the Creator has fashioned everything, especially the human race. To embrace Wisdom is thus to discover the secret of being truly human, of reflecting God's image. This is the secret of the sometimes apparently random book of Proverbs. Wisdom, like Ariadne with her thread, will guide you through the mazes and mysteries of life.

This rich seam of thought, visible at many points in pre-Christian Jewish tradition, is where the early Christians went quarrying for language to deal with the phenomena before them. Long before secular philosophy was used to describe the inner being of the one God, and the relation of this God to Jesus and the Spirit, a vigorous and very Jewish new tradition took the language and imagery of Spirit, Word, Law, Presence (and/or Glory), and Wisdom, and developed them in relation to the Jesus of recent memory and to the strange personal presence of the Spirit. It might be thought that they added a sixth to the list, namely God's Love; except that, for them, God's Love was already no mere personification, a figure of speech for the loving God at work, but a person, the crucified Jesus. Approach the incarnation from this angle, and it is no category mistake, but the utterly appropriate climax of creation. Wisdom, God's blueprint for humans, at last herself becomes human.

Thus Paul can speak repeatedly of God accomplishing his saving and re-creating work *through* Jesus, and of the Spirit as God's personal presence, bringing healing, hope and glory. The inner mutual relationships within the one God have opened up, not only to reveal God in truly human form but to invite all humans to share God's inner life. The Spirit of Truth will take what belongs to Jesus, which is itself the true revelation of the Father, and will share it with Jesus' people. The doctrine of the Trinity is not only the best we can do in speaking of the one God, but also the foundation of Christian spirituality.

Proper 4

——— ∽ ———

1 Kings 18.20–21 [22–29] 30–39
Galatians 1.1–12
Luke 7.1–10

Elijah calls for fire, but the larger story is about rain. Drought has plagued the land. King Ahab is cross with Elijah, blaming the messenger for the message. Elijah, fresh from his triumph in restoring a boy to life (ch. 17), retorts (18.18) that the trouble stems from Ahab himself, who has fostered Baal-worship in Israel. Hence the contest on Carmel. Only when YHWH is acknowledged as the one true God, and Baal-worship is stamped out, will the rains return.

The confrontation is memorable not least for the contrast of styles. There are Baal's prophets, cavorting around their altar, slashing themselves with swords and lances to raise the stakes of sympathetic magic and persuade Baal to do something, but succeeding only in provoking Elijah to splendid scorn (v. 27). And there is Elijah, symbolically evoking the story of Israel's redemption, with the twelve stones, the water, and the fiery presence of God. We think of Elijah as one of the great prophets, and forget that he stood (almost) alone against the mood of the times, constantly having to prove his credentials, constantly recalling the people to the true God.

By the first century, Elijah was seen (along with Phinehas, whose story is found in Numbers 25) as one of the great zealots. Zealous for God and the Law, he opposed paganism within Israel by all means possible, including violence. Many first-century Jews looked to him as a role model, attempting to purify the nation of their day from pagan corruption, disloyalty and idolatry. It seems that Saul of Tarsus took this line, and indeed that this was what took him on his fateful journey to Damascus, to which we shall return next week.

Galatians as a whole, introduced here with dramatic vigour, shows Paul's newly redirected zeal. In the gospel God's truth had been revealed, and he opposed all distortions of it as involving lies about God. Paul saw (v. 4) that in Jesus, and supremely through his death, the 'present evil age' had lost its grip, and that the age to come, the age of freedom and forgiveness long promised by God, had finally arrived.

His great and always paradoxical insight, expounded for the first time in Galatians, was that this action, in fulfilling the promises to Abraham, had created a single family in which all who believed in Jesus, Jews and Gentiles alike, belonged together with nothing but their faith as the badge of membership. Any attempt to co-opt the story of Jesus for a 'gospel' which left Jewish ethnic privilege intact he regarded as a spurious pseudo-gospel, and opposed with Elijah-like zeal.

Luke's account of the centurion and his servant makes very nearly the same point. Not even in Israel has such faith been found. No need to dance around and use pagan-style sympathetic magic. Jesus, like a new Elijah, raises the lad from death, demonstrating for those with eyes to see where the living God is now at work.

Proper 5

―― ∿ ――

1 Kings 17.8–24
Galatians 1.11–24
Luke 7.11–17

Luke has, fairly obviously, told the story of the widow's son at Nain in such a way as to evoke the similar story of Elijah and the widow's son at Zarephath – who, interestingly, was already referred to in Jesus' 'Nazareth manifesto' (4.26). Luke elsewhere makes it clear that Jesus is to be seen as Messiah, and indeed more than Messiah. This does not exclude, but rather takes up within itself, the fact that he was first and foremost seen as 'a prophet mighty in word and deed' (24.19). This is one of many stories that prepares the way for that conclusion, simultaneously tying Jesus in to the long story of Israel and showing him bringing that story to its triumphant climax.

The point about such actions is not merely that they demonstrated remarkable power, but that they validated the prophet's work. The story of the Zarephath widow is one of increasing faith: she initially has enough faith in Elijah to bake him a little cake before she provides for herself and her son; she interprets the boy's death in terms of Elijah having brought judgement on her (for what reason, we are not told); but she finally acknowledges him wholeheartedly as a man of God, and his words as the true words of YHWH. The implication is that she, unlike those hardened in unbelief in Luke 16.31, now believes fully on the evidence of one being raised from the dead. In the same way, the Nain story enables Luke to point forward to his own resurrection narrative when the prophet/Messiah himself emerges the other side of death, thereby retrospectively validating all he had earlier done and said.

The centrality of Jesus, and the revelation of God's redemptive accomplishment in him, lies at the heart of Paul's passionate defence of his gospel. He insists – against, we must assume, slurs and innuendoes emanating from opponents – that his apostolic commission went back to Jesus himself, rather than being a second-order affair dependent on the Jerusalem church. Galatia cannot, in other words, appeal over his head to Jerusalem. The only person Paul answers to is Jesus himself.

The language in which Paul describes his conversion carries ironic reference to Elijah, this time to 1 Kings 19. Like the prophet, he had been very zealous for the Lord, but found himself confronted with a fresh revelation that made him go off to Arabia – to Mount Sinai, we should probably assume – so that like Elijah he might hand in his commission, might give up zeal as a bad job. However, like Elijah, he is given a new commission. A new king is to be proclaimed. The Son of God is to be revealed in him and through him (v. 16). His zeal is to be transformed and re-directed. Like the widow at Zarephath, Paul sees in Jesus' resurrection the complete evidence that he has not only brought sins to light but has triumphantly dealt with the judgement that they incurred.

Proper 6

—— ∼ ——

1 Kings 21.1–21a
Galatians 2.15–21
Luke 7.36—8.3

'He loved me and gave himself for me.' These words in Galatians 2.20, coupled with those in 1.4, probably form the earliest written statement of what we know as the doctrine of the atonement. They invite comment at several levels.

First, towering over everything else, they speak of the cross as an act of love. Paul is sometimes wrongly supposed to have seen the cross solely through legalistic lenses, imagining it as an exercise in penal logic-chopping. This passage demonstrates that for him it was far more, and far deeper. It spoke of arms outstretched in love, a heart bursting for love, the self-giving of love to the undeserving beloved. It created, in the words of the late George Caird, 'a debt of love which only love could repay'.

Second, when coupled with 1.4 the phrase speaks of a once-for-all action in which Jesus, as Israel's Messiah, brought Israel and the world round the corner of history from darkness to light. Though the cross speaks to the heart of the individual believer, it does so in the context of a cosmic achievement through which the shape of reality is permanently changed. A new world has been born, with the word 'Forgiveness' pinned over its cradle. This was the work of 'the Son of God': a messianic title which, as Paul discovered, was filled with astonishing new content. Some of

Israel's ancient rulers, exemplified all too well by Ahab, were happy to kill those who stood in their way, revealing a totally misguided sense of what Israel and her kings were there for. The true King of the Jews embodies the loving presence, and dying love, of Israel's true God.

Third, as the verses immediately before today's passage make clear, the first practical implication of the cross is that the self-giving love that has created the new family must be worked out in the family's table manners. Jewish Christians and Gentile Christians no longer belong in separate categories, at separate tables. As well as being the earliest statement of the atonement, this passage is Paul's first statement of 'justification by faith'; and here it means, quite simply, that since all believers are already full members of God's people, without having to 'qualify' by keeping the Jewish law, they all belong together at the same meal.

All this is of course superbly and dramatically expressed, in narrative form, in today's Gospel. Here is the table, with the Pharisee playing host (though not very enthusiastically); here is the woman, excluded from fellowship; here is the Son of God, loving and giving himself – incurring wrath already, already sensing the shadow of the cross – and opening the new world of forgiveness. Here is the debt of love, repaid by love so extravagantly as to reveal how great the debt actually was. The somewhat troubling question is, of course: which of the two characters addressed by Jesus would be more at home in our churches this Sunday?

Proper 7

———— ∾ ————

1 Kings 19.1–15a
Galatians 3.23–end
Luke 8.26–39

Elijah went to Sinai, to hand back his commission. 'I've done all this for you, and now they're going to kill me. I've had enough.' Fear and exhaustion generated self-destructive depression. What was he expecting? A volcanic eruption, literal or theological? A new set of commandments? The renewal of the covenant with him personally, as God had once suggested to Moses?

Instead, a challenge: 'What are you doing here, Elijah?' How much of your problem is self-caused, the reverse side of zealous energy? If your weapon in God's service has been destructive anger, don't be surprised if, when things get tough, it turns back on yourself. In any case, depression, as usual, has distorted your perception of reality. God has the situation well in hand (vv. 15–18): new kings and prophets are to be anointed, and will sort things out. Elijah is not the only true Israelite. Seven thousand others have not worshipped Baal. Elijah wanted a new or renewed law. He received the command to trust and obey.

Paul was familiar with the Elijah stories, and in his pre-conversion days seems to have made them his role model, casting himself as the fiery prophet and the Christians as the new Baal-worshippers. After his conversion he, too, went off to Arabia to do business with God, and came back with a new commission, to announce the anointed one, the Messiah.

With hindsight, he saw the law of Sinai quite differently. It had looked after the Israelites, had (like a slave in charge of the children) administered rough justice to stop them going to the bad. The law had, in particular, prevented the family of Abraham compromising its unique vision and vocation by mingling with paganism.

But with the coming of the crucified Messiah all that has changed. The Messiah is now the focal point of God's people: all who believe in God's unique action through him are therefore part of the family. Abraham's promised offspring now consists of all, Jew and Gentile alike, who share this faith. (The Galatians were tempted to reinforce the superiority of Jew over Gentile; Paul, addressing this, does not develop his throwaway line, that the gospel also brings together slave and free, male and female.)

Paul even (in the next chapter) likens the rule of the Law over Israel to that of idols over the pagans. God's action in the Messiah has liberated Jew and Gentile alike from their former deadly bondage. The baptismal symbolism makes the point (3.27): coming up out of the water, both have put on identical clothes, marking their new identity. Like the Gerasene demoniac, they have watched Jesus destroy the demons which had enslaved them, and now find themselves sitting at his feet, clothed and in their right mind. Like him, too (Luke 8.39), they will now find that when they try to tell people what God has done for them, they somehow always speak of what Jesus has done for them.

Proper 8

— ∽ —

2 Kings 2.1–14
Galatians 5.1, 13–25
Luke 9.51–end

'Leave the dead to bury their dead.' One of Jesus' starkest commands, this flies in the face of the sacred Jewish obligation to attend to the burial of one's father ahead of all other duties, even saying one's daily prayers. Jesus' kingdom-announcement is so urgent, so unique, that it must either be followed, grasped and proclaimed totally or lost altogether. The family, a central and vital symbol of the people of God, is thus radically redefined. Following Jesus at once is the only thing that counts.

Elijah, by contrast, seems bent on dissuading Elisha from following him. 'Stay here; I'm going on.' But Elisha refuses: 'As the Lord lives, I won't leave you.' His doggedness is rewarded. Foxes have holes, the birds of the air nests, but prophets have nowhere to call home. Instead, Elisha inherits a double share of Elijah's spirit, the great wind of God that will blow through Israel and cleanse it from corruption, the fire that will burn away the dross.

The stories of Elijah and Elisha were alive and well in Jesus' day, and caused confusion to the disciples as well as to readers of the Gospels. When first called by Elijah, Elisha had asked permission to say goodbye to his family, and it had apparently been granted, however briefly (1 Kings 19.19–21). Elijah, faced with opposition, called down fire from heaven, but when the disciples volunteered to try the same trick they were firmly rebuked. The Spirit who spoke by the prophets is now speaking through the Son, and the wind and fire are to be found in him, in his urgent kingdom-message, in his pilgrimage to Jerusalem and in what he will there accomplish. What is now required is not the zeal that will burn up the opposition, but the Spirit of Jesus to transform those who follow him doggedly wherever he goes. 'As the Lord lives, I won't leave you'; to those who speak thus to him, Jesus will reply in the same words.

The two types of zeal emerge graphically in Galatians. The Jewish Christian 'agitators', with their zeal for the Jewish law, are causing anger and tension within the young Church. By treating the ex-pagan Christians as still outside the true family circle, they are in effect forcing them to become proselytes. But the family has been redefined, by Jesus with his radical kingdom-achievement, and now by Paul with his insistence that faith, not the Jewish law, is the badge of membership. As a result, with considerable irony, insistence on the Jewish law will result in living 'according to the flesh', in bitterness and division, putting such Christians on a level with those who follow the usual pagan 'fleshly' lifestyle. The only way forward is to inherit in full measure the Spirit of Jesus, passing beyond the divisive rule of the Jewish law, into the realm where the wind blows where it wants, and the fire of love burns away all the dross.

Proper 9

———— ❧ ————

2 Kings 5.1–14
Galatians 6.1–16
Luke 10.1–11, 16–20

Going out like lambs amid wolves hardly makes sense in any culture. Only Jesus could propose something so apparently hare-brained yet strangely powerful. Only he, knowing himself to be utterly vulnerable, yet protected by his Father, could suggest the same course to others. Despite certain opposition, misunderstanding, threats and outright rejection (the squeamish lectionary predictably soft-pedals the latter theme), Jesus' seventy chosen ones will go out in weakness, and yet in power, as a sign to Israel that the kingdom is breaking in, the kingdom at whose approach the dark enemy, the Satan himself, will fall in terror.

Behind the challenge and the commission there stands, of course, Jesus' own sense of vocation, of what was happening and was about to happen in and through his own work. Yearning for the kingdom, Israel was nevertheless not ready for the kingdom-vision he had to bring, had to enact. Every moment, though, was precious; hence the strategy of sending heralds ahead of him, to proclaim his peace and prepare his way. Jesus' mission was urgent, since those who rejected his way of peace, his alternative vision of how God would sweep through the world with justice and love, would find they had spurned their last chance. Everyone had to hear while there was time.

No slouch when it came to urgency, Paul challenges the Galatians one more time to think straight, to resist the blandishments of those who offered a softer, safer version of the gospel. Nothing less than the full article will do: the world crucified to me, and I to the world. If you walk by this rule, you will find peace, just as will those who welcomed Jesus' emissaries; but if you modify it you court disaster. Everything may seem to be against you. Lambs among wolves describes quite closely how many of the early converts, in Galatia and elsewhere, must have felt. Losing all to gain Christ: that was the message of the cross, of the gospel, of the new creation.

If these stirring reflections are to mean anything now, they must address the problem: what are the urgent questions upon which major issues hang at this moment? Only those who have struggled hard with such matters know how difficult it is to judge, to decide when to be 'prophetic' and speak out, how to tell the difference between a storm in a teacup and a force ten hurricane. Take Elisha, for instance; he recognized that, if Naaman's pride was humbled, and his leprosy healed, by Israel's God, he, the great enemy commander, would remain loyal to this God, and hence presumably be unwilling to fight against Israel, despite apparent compromise (bowing himself down in the house of Rimmon; do, please, read the whole story). Turn the question around, though, and look at Gehazi, Elisha's servant; for him it was all a trivial affair, something merely to be turned to his own personal advantage. Lucky the church whose prophets have their heads screwed on.

Proper 10

——— ～ ———

Amos 7.7–17
Colossians 1.1–14
Luke 10.25–37

If you like word-development, you'll love Samaritans. Start with a geographical designation: people who live in the hill country, between Galilee and Judaea. Develop to discrimination: the pre-exilic Judaeans speaking of their northern neighbours, the people who are like us but not quite. Then post-exilic denunciation: the wrong sort, with the wrong worship, the wrong theology and the wrong behaviour. Then re-evaluation, initiated by Jesus (so far as we know, one of his most unprecedented innovations): people who might perhaps love God and their neighbour across traditional boundaries, and who might therefore come within the pale after all. Then, much later (the dictionary offers 1649 as the earliest occurrence), a real evolution: those who, not necessarily outsiders, rescue people in need. The derived sense, the shocking surprise in Jesus' day, has become, for most users, the word's only meaning.

The parable has suffered, along with the word, from being too well known. It isn't, after all, simply about helping half-dead dogs over stiles. It's about Jesus' major re-evaluation of Israel's boundary-markers. The lawyer quoted the *Shema*, the central Jewish prayer, as the litmus test for inheriting the Age to Come: love God, love your neighbour. The parable, redefining 'neighbour', doesn't conclude that the man in need was the Samaritan's neighbour, but that the Samaritan was his. The challenge is not just to copy the Samaritan, but to recognize him when he comes to our aid.

The dark side of the story is, of course, that the priest and the levite turned out not to be neighbours after all. Like those attacked by Amos, they were so interested in protecting their own status that could not see what that status – being the official representatives of the people of God – was all about, and so were actually jeopardizing it. The priest who attacked Amos ('Chapel Royal: No Prophets Allowed') was the true ancestor of Jesus' anonymous passers-by, only in his case he could not see that it was the nation as a whole that was lying half dead in the ditch, needing to be stirred into life by Amos's denunciations. When God declares that Israel doesn't measure up, and the prophet who passes the message on is labelled a conspirator, the only possible answer is condemnation.

But that isn't God's last word. When Paul greets the young church in Colosse, the feature of their new life to which he draws attention is 'your love in the spirit' (1.8). Paul, in prison (in Ephesus, in my humble but probably accurate opinion), hears from his colleague Epaphras, not that certain people have had wonderful spiritual experiences, not that they have learnt a textbook of systematic theology, but that there has come into existence in Colosse a community of people who love one another across traditional boundaries (compare 3.11). This event has the fingerprints of God all over it. For 'Samaritan', read 'Colossian'. Why not give another word a push in the right direction?

Proper 11

— ❧ —

Amos 8.1–12
Colossians 1.15–28
Luke 10.38–end

Put Paul alongside Mary and Martha, and which one does he remind you of? 'For this I toil', he writes, 'and struggle with all the energy that Christ powerfully inspires within me.' More like Martha? Yes and no. It has been customary to play the two sisters off, passive spirituality versus aggressive fussiness. Mary wins, but at a cost: as feminists point out, this model keeps both in the neat boxes devised by a male world, the one sedate and devout, the other making the tea and sandwiches.

The reality is more complex. People sat at a teacher's feet in that world, not to gaze languidly with drooping eyelids, but in order to become teachers themselves. Paul, after all, had 'sat at the feet of Gamaliel', and that hadn't made him exactly passive. Mary had crossed a boundary, entering the man's world of discipleship; Jesus had affirmed her right to be there, indeed the desirability of her being there rather than simply staying in the kitchen. Once Mary had drunk in the rich teaching of Jesus, she too would be on her feet, but not simply in the background.

Paul's energy was not simply a character trait. It was the surging new life of one who had worshipped at the feet of Jesus. Colossians, steeped in the adoration of Jesus the image, the first-born, the head, the reconciler, the fullness of

God, is also a practical, down-to-earth letter, energetically getting on with the job.

Paul was commissioned 'to make the word of God fully known' (1.25). When Amos inveighs against social injustice, economic trickery and exploitation in Israel, the most terrible of his threats (8.11–12) is that there is to be a famine, not of bread, but of the word of YHWH. A vivid picture of panic: people wandering to and fro, running this way and that, longing for the word of YHWH and not finding it. Those who turn their back on the written word, that commands justice, sabbath-keeping, and care for the poor, will find the spoken word has gone silent on them as well. Paul's gospel, against this background, is the answer to the secret but desperate longing of the heart: the image of the invisible God, the sound of the inaudible God, the touch of the untouchable God.

Which is why, we may presume, this gospel is proclaimed in the midst of, and indeed acted out in and through, suffering. When the world has gone its own way, trampling on the needy, cheating on weights and measures, casting God's wise ordering of life out of the way so that it can make another quick buck, the word of grace is bound to cause a different sort of panic. If that stuff were to get around, profits would drop. Not for nothing does Paul celebrate the fact that Christ is Lord of the principalities and powers. Sit at the feet of this teacher, and you will find work soon enough.

Proper 12

— ∼ —

Hosea 1.2–10
Colossians 2.6–19
Luke 11.1–13

Part of the prophetic vocation seems to have been to carry the pain of the message in one's own soul. Thus it was, at least, with Hosea. Married to a prostitute, he felt not only the pain of Israel but also the pain of God, seeing his people cavorting off after other gods. His children were and weren't his own, just as Israel was and wasn't God's child. Self-induced judgement loomed over them, but yearning love followed as well: 'not my people' will again be addressed as 'children of the living God'.

The fatherhood of the true God undergirds Jesus' announcement of the kingdom, together with the spirituality he encouraged and the bracing moral agenda he urged. Not every parable can be pressed to yield an accurate account of God (the 'unjust judge' is the classic example), but fatherhood is Jesus' most common image for God, woven into every other story. Rooted as it is in the biblical picture of God's rescue of Israel from Egypt in the first place and from oppression thereafter, this image does not so much pin God down with a particular cultural family role as open up a window on his character. He wears his heart on his sleeve, providing for his children and coming to their rescue when they are in distress. To recognize who this God is is at once to be welcomed into a spirituality of pure trust (who was it

90

who used to say 'I must speak to Father about this'?), even when the request is apparently unreasonable. Prayer that begins, 'Father, hallowed be your name', can continue, in that treasured mixture of intimacy and awe, into the details of the three loaves suddenly necessary at midnight.

It is because Paul had seen this God revealed in Jesus Christ that he realized, with deep sorrow, that his own fellow Jews, by rejecting their Messiah, have forgotten their true God. Despite scholarly traditions, Colossians 2 is not warning against a strange esoteric super-spirituality, but against the blandishments of Judaism itself. The emphasis of the chapter is: you have already been circumcised in Christ (2.11–12), and the law has no more condemnation against you (2.13–15). Christ's paradoxical triumph over the principalities and powers included the law itself, in so far as it set a bar against Gentiles, 'not God's people', being deemed, in Christ, 'children of the living God'. When he says (2.8) 'Don't let anyone lure you astray by philosophy and empty deceit', he is deliberately using pagan language to describe the attractions of Judaism to the pagan world: he uses the very rare Greek word *sylagogon* for 'lure you astray', with the punning hint 'Don't let anyone *synagogue* you'.

For Paul, of course, this was extremely painful. As he says in Romans, he carried the tragedy of Israel's situation in his own heart and soul. But also the joy of knowing God at a deeper level: in Christ 'all God's fullness dwells bodily' (2.9).

Proper 13

— ∾ —

Hosea 11.1–11
Colossians 3.1–11
Luke 12.13–21

Many years ago I preached a sermon on Luke 12. Jesus did not come, I declared, to settle our property disputes. Pleased with my own eloquence, I came home to find a note from my neighbour, pinned to the back door, telling me that my garden shed encroached on his land and that if it wasn't moved soon he would bulldoze it. He was probably in the wrong, but the irony stung too badly. I moved the shed.

But if Jesus didn't come to settle our disputes, nor does this passage simply refer to everyday stories of garden sheds. Land, and ancestral inheritance thereon, was of course one of Judaism's central symbols, then as now. Getting it right was part of obedience to God's will, and moreover focused the glittering promise of return from exile, as Hosea and so many others had promised. The God who called Israel, his little son, out of Egypt, will call his trembling exiles, from the ends of the world, back to their native land.

But God's people have always lived in the tension between vocation and the symbols which express it. Cling to the symbol, and you risk disobeying the vocation – and forfeiting the reality. The fool who pulled down his barns to build bigger ones, only to be summoned to leave it all behind, is not just a symbol for, well, a rich fool who ... did precisely that. If that were the case, the story wouldn't be a parable, but merely a moral tale. The real target was the Israel that prided herself on national security, claiming more and more territory, ancestral and otherwise, not realizing that her God was asking questions at another level altogether, summoning her back to being the light of the world, ordering her national life with justice and mercy and becoming a beacon of hope to the nations. How can being the people of God be ultimately a matter of sacred turf, if Israel is to be the light of the whole world? How can litigious and grasping behaviour reflect the generous and forgiving love of God?

The stern warnings are meant to act, as Hosea says, as the roaring of the lion that drives Israel back to her God. Paul is quite capable of the same tactic, but in Colossians 3 he takes a different route. Being dead and risen with Christ, we are to seek that which is above, not that which is on the earth. This, as the succeeding verses make clear, is not a recipe for a super-spirituality which ignores the real earthy issues. First things first: the problem is not living on earth, but living *on earth's terms*. Make this earth your god (as even Israel was tempted to do, by idolizing her God-given symbols), and you end up with lies, anger, greed and immorality, the property disputes of the present world. The Creator, meanwhile, serves notice of a higher calling: a full, true humanness, remade in his own image.

Proper 14

———— ∾ ————

Isaiah 1.1, 10–20
Hebrews 11.1–3, 8–16
Luke 12.32–40

Stories about a master going away and returning would have been interpreted in Jesus' world as stories about Israel's God, YHWH. He had 'gone away' at the exile, as Ezekiel describes graphically. At no point in the 'post-exilic' literature does anyone say that he has returned; but at almost every point it insists that he will. When he does, it will mean not just blessing, but judgement.

The later prophets retain Isaiah's sense that Israel's God has a controversy with his people. Things can be argued out, sins can be forgiven, but the first word may well be one of rebuke. 'People of Sodom and Gomorrah', indeed! Shock tactics to bring the people to their senses, lest God come and discover them deep in self-indulgence, violence, exploitation, and the religion that puts on airs to cover it all up. Isaiah's warnings are worryingly perennial.

The stories Jesus told about a returning master would therefore be heard primarily as stories about the expected return of God to judge his people, and they make excellent sense on that basis. The kingdom is coming, when God will return and put all things to rights; so those who follow Jesus, and are thereby constituted as the real Israel, are to trust his imminent provision rather than store up for themselves. Like servants who know what their master will want them to be doing, they obey without knowing when he will arrive.

Into this story and exhortation (Luke 12.35–38, 41–48), Luke has inserted (12.39–40) a different snippet about a different 'coming'. Now the owner is at home, and the one who comes is a thief; within Jesus' kaleidoscopic imagery, this could simply be highlighting the imminent danger as well as the reward, but it looks like a separate theme. In the application (v. 40) it is 'the Son of man' who is 'coming'. Elsewhere, the coming of the Son of Man, as in Daniel 7, is his vindicated coming *from* earth, after persecution, *to* God in heaven. But, again in Daniel 7, with that vindication goes judgement for those who have opposed God's kingdom. This dense little saying warns of imminent catastrophe: Jesus will be vindicated, but those who are not ready will find the day coming upon them like a thief in the night.

Hebrews holds up the patriarchs (and matriarchs) as examples of faith: living in the light of the future, they were ready for it when it came. The coming heavenly country is not far off and disembodied; it is the sphere, already existing and very close, in which God's purposes are stored up, like scenery ready for the stage. Citizens of this new city live already by its customs, secure in the knowledge that, though they look strange now and here, they will make sense then and there. When the master comes, he will recognize them as his own. More, he will not be ashamed, says Hebrews, to be called 'their God'. '*Their*'?

Proper 15

—— ~~ ——

Isaiah 5.1–7
Hebrews 11.29—12.2
Luke 12.49–56

This Lukan passage is high on the list of Things We Would Rather Jesus Hadn't Said. It's not gentle, it's not meek and mild; it's not even nice. Parents and children at loggerheads, in-laws getting across one another – what can Jesus have had in mind?

The problem, as often, is that we fail to pick up the biblical allusion. Micah's picture (7.6) of family dysfunction is part of his lament about his contemporaries. Like the suffering heroes of Hebrews 11, the prophet continues to trust in God (7.7) and his coming rescue. He looked by faith, Hebrews would say, to God's future, now finally revealed in Jesus himself, the example of our faith and the object of our hope. But to those who refuse this faith and hope, this same Jesus declares that he has come, prophet-like, to divide Israel down the middle. If the vineyard is yielding wild grapes, what else is the owner to do?

People know how to read the sky, so why can't they see what is going on under their noses? What is Jesus referring to? Positively: his kingdom-message was bursting in with the love and power of God, healing, rescuing, re-creating; people who couldn't draw the right conclusions must be blind indeed. Negatively: those who rejected his message would come into increasing conflict with Rome, a conflict in which there could be only one winner – not just because of the power of Rome, but because Israel would be fighting the battle without the support of her God. Jesus was urging his contemporaries to a way of being Israel which meant peace and justice. To reject his message was to choose the way of self-destruction. In reading the signs of the times, there was no room for mere optimists or pessimists. The greatest blessing and the greatest disaster ever known were both just around the corner.

The next little saying (12.57–59), sadly omitted by the lectionary, belongs exactly in this train of thought. It is another example of something usually taken as a bit of homely wisdom, when in fact it is a dark parable, like Isaiah's strange vineyard-song. Reading the times meant recognizing that Israel was about to be hauled into court; she should settle now, while there was still time, before suffering the ultimate penalty. But even as he said this, Jesus, like Isaiah, knew what the answer would be.

Why then is Isaiah's vineyard-oracle called a *love*-song? The vineyard was a well-known metaphor for a bride, to be loved, looked after, fruitful, enjoyed. Isaiah's hearers would expect a wedding song, and would be shocked. But it was a love song none the less: the lament of YHWH's grieving love over his cherished but rebellious people, a love that would be satisfied with nothing less than embodiment, to share and bear the baptism of fire, to take upon itself the bad news to make the good come true at last.

Proper 16

—— ∽ ——

Jeremiah 1.4–10
Hebrews 12.18–end
Luke 13.10–17

Moses said he wasn't a speaker. Isaiah said his lips were tainted. Ezekiel fell on his face. And Jeremiah says he's too young. One might, perhaps, be a trifle suspicious if God's call to prophecy met with too ready a response: 'Oh yes, that's fine, I think I can do a good job...'? Hmmm.

This isn't just appropriate humility (which can itself easily be counterfeited: as they say about sincerity, that when you can fake that you've really got it made, so with humility, when you can turn that on, you've really got something to be proud of). It's a matter of the sheer scale of the task, like being asked to climb the north wall of the Eiger in bare feet. It means standing trembling before the living God, in order to stand boldly before the world. Unless one has been overwhelmed by the size of this task, one hasn't been paying attention. This isn't genteel modesty. It's horror and panic.

God outflanked all Jeremiah's objections. He was marked out before conception, consecrated before birth. God's protecting presence would be with him (if 'don't be afraid' is the most frequent biblical command, 'I am with you', which regularly backs it up, is one of the most frequent of the biblical promises). God would supply him with the necessary words; the Lord of the nations would appoint him as his spokesman to the rulers of the world. Yes, there would be much negative work ('pluck up, pull down, destroy, overthrow'), but building and planting would follow. Chosen, commissioned, commanded, equipped, supported, comforted, encouraged, the young Jeremiah sets off on a career that will break him and make him.

The contrast Hebrews draws between the fearsome Mount Sinai and the joys of the heavenly Jerusalem should not make us imagine for a moment that the new covenant replaces terror with cosiness. Reverence and awe before the consuming fire is reaffirmed in the New Testament as the appropriate stance for any believer; how much more, for those called to stand humbly in God's presence in order then to speak boldly to the rulers of this age. Hebrews offers both context and hope: our life is conducted, whether we realize it or not, before the angels, archangels and all the company of heaven, and the one whom we serve has committed himself to 'shaking' heaven and earth once more, in order to establish a kingdom that cannot be shaken. We go to our Christian tasks surrounded by invisible witnesses, assured that the work we do belongs to that future unshakeable realm.

The one in whose presence we stand is now known, not just as consuming fire, but as Jesus. In every gospel reading, not least this one, we see another facet of his own prophetic call, humbly obedient to God's will, sternly opposed to the rulers of this age, gently building and planting new life, new hope. The way to discover contemporary vocation is to stand in his presence, trembling but obedient.

Proper 17

—— ❧ ——

Jeremiah 2.4–13
Hebrews 13.1–8, 15–16
Luke 14.1, 7–14

Don't sit at the top table, declares Jesus; start at the bottom and see what happens. If this is a parable, as Luke says, it isn't advice about behaviour at dinner parties. In Luke's wider context, its meaning is cognate with Jesus' warning and summons to his contemporaries. God has promised a great wedding party, the 'messianic banquet'. But if Israel thinks she has an inalienable right to sit at the top table, she has another think coming. Pride comes before a fall, humility before exaltation. This isn't just wise counsel to an individual: it's Jesus' great challenge to the Israel of his day.

However, since Jesus Christ is 'the same yesterday and today and for ever', it is right that we apply the message to other days, other places. We dare not restrict it to the cameo portrait of prudent social humility. Jesus worked with a bigger canvas. His message, focused now on his cross and resurrection, summons the powers of the world to humility; those who think themselves great are confronted with their own true King shamefully executed, a sight which overturns all arrogance and unmasks all pretension. Faced with the crucified and risen Lord of the world, the rulers of the nations will begin with shame to take the lowest place.

Hebrews 13 outlines the lifestyle of those who have based their lives on the humiliating gospel of Jesus. Hospitality renounces pride of home and family; identifying with political prisoners renounces pride of social status. The false gods of sex and money, who puff up their devotees with a spurious haughtiness, are renounced in chastity and humble trust. Worship the true God, and share the good things you have. This humble way of living, pleasing to God, embodying the reality to which the Temple cult pointed, will call down abuse and threats from those whose own lifestyles are thereby exposed as arrogant, but this merely reinforces the fact that the present world is not our ultimate home. 'We seek the city that is to come.' In that city, pride and fear are replaced by gratitude and trust.

Half a millennium before Jesus, Jeremiah launched his first scathing rebuke to the Jews of his day. What has God done, he asks, to deserve this treatment from his own people? Not only are they elbowing their way to the top table, but when they get there they treat it as if it were their own, not God's at all – and then, having created an empty god-slot, they fill it with worthless alternative divinities. Instead of gratitude for redemption, they exhibit arrogance and abomination. Priests, rulers and prophets alike go along with it. Not only have they left the flowing spring of clear water to dig out cisterns for themselves; the cisterns they have dug are cracked and useless.

Translate this challenge, through the medium of Jesus' parable, to the world and Church of today. And make sure the medium – the way you say it – matches the message.

Proper 18

—— ～ ——

Jeremiah 18.1–11
Philemon 1–21
Luke 14.25–33

Luke 14 has more than its fair share of 'hard sayings'. Hate your family; give up your possessions. A nice clear message for the end of the summer holidays. And, to back it up, a solemn warning: such carrying the cross requires clear-eyed calculation and commitment, like someone building a tower or fighting a battle. Half measures will fail, and fail shamefully.

Before we give this the salt-water treatment – first you water it down, then you take it with a pinch of salt – we should recognize its first-century local colour and focus.

Building the Temple and fighting God's battle constituted the messianic task. Herod the Great began to rebuild the Temple; by Jesus' day it was two-thirds complete. It was to be both the dwelling of God on earth and the legitimation of Herod's family as kings of the Jews. Jesus, however, had come as the true king, to build, indeed to be, the real Temple. Were his followers ready to pay the price? Jesus' contemporaries wanted to fight Rome and gain their freedom, winning God's victory over the pagan hordes. Jesus, however, had come to fight the real battle against the real enemy. Were his followers ready to enlist?

The challenge of Jesus' double project would involve cutting ties with current Jewish symbols and aspirations.

The family lay at the heart of Judaism; but Jesus was creating a new family around himself. The land, the most important possession, constituted Israel as a geographical entity; but Jesus' mission, though focused on the nation, had in view the whole of God's world. Those who followed him would therefore incur the wrath both of their Jewish contemporaries, for going soft on nationalist agendas, and of Rome, for launching a kingdom-movement. Carrying the cross was not a metaphor in Jesus' day. To apply this passage, consider the symbols and aspirations by which our own society steers its course.

God was doing at last, on a grand scale, what Jeremiah had predicted. The clay was being put back on the wheel, to be reworked into another vessel. Same clay, new pot: a vital, teasing image of the continuity and discontinuity that comes about when God's chosen and beloved people rebel. The clay cannot complain. The potter is not arbitrary or whimsical, but is responding in creative love to the failure of the first pot. (Like all images, this one eventually breaks down; but it must be allowed to make its point.)

For similar reasons, Paul appeals to Philemon on behalf of his runaway slave Onesimus. God has not finished with the lad, and is making something new of him. To recognize this will mean a huge effort of rethinking on Philemon's part, not unlike that to which Jesus was challenging his followers: instead of a piece of property, Onesimus is a human being for whom the Messiah died. Feel free to read verse 22 as well, and ponder why Paul told Philemon to prepare him a guest room.

Proper 19

—— ∾ ——

Jeremiah 4.11–28
1 Timothy 1.12–17
Luke 15.1–10

In a recent article, a priest from another tradition described the cheerful mixture of spiritualities which made up his regular personal prayer. It was a vivid and moving account of a busy man nourishing and cherishing a sense of God's presence through thick and thin. But at the end my blood ran cold. He often failed, he said; 'but since the Lord has enabled me to base myself on this structure of prayer', he concluded, 'I hope and believe He will save me, as and when He chooses.'

Well, the New Testament does speak of the witness of the Spirit, assuring us in our prayers that we are God's children and that his love will embrace us eternally. But the way he put it was misleading. How might the parable go? 'Supposing you have a hundred sheep, and a good number of them come to base themselves on a structure of feeding and resting which will be good for them; will you not bring those ones safely to the sheepfold at last?'

What was it, after all, about that one lost sheep that made the shepherd go after it? It wasn't the one with the woolliest coat. It wasn't the one with the sweet, almost human bleat. It wasn't the one that regularly nuzzled up close to his knees. It was simply the one that was lost. No qualification except a disqualification. No structure to its life, no good sense, no obedience. That was the one that got the ride home on the shepherd's shoulders. That was the one that made the angels sing for joy.

All right; of course the sheep could say, on the way home, 'I know I'm being saved, because I'm riding on the shepherd's shoulders.' But the gospel message upon which our hope is based is not about the ride home, but about the good shepherd's journey into the wilderness, a journey undertaken out of sheer love and completed with sheer joy. If this is what makes the whole company of heaven sing, then when we join with them at each eucharist we must celebrate it too. Any suggestion that we contribute something to our own rescue is like advising someone going up in a lift to take a ladder as well, just in case.

Paul saw the crazy logic of the shepherd's action. He wasn't just a lost sheep; he was a wolf, harrying and devouring the flock. But even he received mercy, so that he might serve as an example. If he could be rescued, anyone could. Rescued, though, from what? Jeremiah's classic description of life in the wilderness, rebelling against the shepherd's care and love, says it all. 'My people are foolish; they do not know me; skilled in doing evil, they have no idea how to do good.' The result: creation itself deconstructs, goes back to being 'without form and void'. The angels sing when a sinner is rescued by grace; heaven and earth mourn when God's people go astray.

Proper 20

—— ∾ ——

Jeremiah 8.18—9.1
1 Timothy 2.1–7
Luke 16.1–13

The first thing to get clear about the 'parable of the wicked mammon' is that it is precisely a *parable*. It is not advice about financial management: Jesus is not telling people to cheat their bosses. It makes sense within Jesus' Jewish context on the one hand and Luke's on the other.

Rabbinic parables about a master and a steward are about God and Israel. Jesus regularly charges his contemporaries with infidelity to their commission: called to be the light of the world, they have kept the light for themselves, and have turned it into darkness. One symptom of this, evidenced in the previous chapter, is that Jesus' opponents have become so concerned about keeping what they see as their master's regulations that they cannot accept that Jesus' welcome of the poor and the outcast reflects the master's real intentions. Like the elder brother in the previous parable, or the hard-hearted miser in the next one, they risk being shut out from the master's household, being put out of their stewardship. Jesus, like Jeremiah, is warning of an awesome imminent disaster, whose approach calls all standard practice into question.

What should they do? Throw caution to the winds, and embody the generous love of the master for all and sundry. The parable may hint at some local colour: the steward was perhaps remitting interest (which the master should not have been levying) rather than capital. The master could not charge him with fraud without exposing himself as a usurer. But the thrust remains: judgement is coming upon God's steward-people, and it is time for them to make what arrangements they can with the wider world, with the outcasts and the Gentiles, forgetting the minutiae of the law, and the commitment to family and property. Ancestral land, no longer 'holy', has become 'unrighteous mammon', and is best used for the good of the new community, the one which the master is paradoxically calling into being through the gospel.

The moral teaching that follows (vv. 10–13) applies this more specifically. The early Church shared property, not simply as an exercise in ancient communism, but as a symbolic act: God's people were no longer defined by sacred land. Luke's fusion of this material (what was the elder brother really cross about?) throws into sharp relief his continuing challenge to the Christian community to embody God's generous welcome to all those who need the good news.

The overtones ring through into 1 Timothy. First-century Jews and Christians faced the question: granted that, as good monotheists, we must not offer sacrifice to the Emperor, what line should we take? Call down a curse on him instead? The mainstream early Church (like many Jews) said: no, we must pray for him, and for all officials. This is not just political prudence. It is based on the same covenantal monotheism that underlies Luke 16. The master loves the world outside, and wants stewards who will seek its salvation, not merely their own.

Proper 21

—— ~ ——

Jeremiah 32.1–15
1 Timothy 6.6–19
Luke 16.19–end

Among the many symbolic actions Jeremiah was commanded to perform, this one stands out as a sign, not of
judgement, but of hope: hope for God's restoration the other
side of judgement. Resurrection hope, if you like. He is
commanded to put his money where his mouth has been
(Jeremiah 31 predicts God's new covenant with Israel): in the
teeth of enemy invasion and imminent disaster, he is to buy a
field. I am reminded of Martin Luther, who declared that if
he knew the kingdom of God was to come tomorrow, he
would go out and plant a tree.

God's future, breaking into and making sense of the
present, is the subject of this week's Lukan parable. Again
we must remind ourselves that this is not literal teaching.
Most of Jesus' hearers already believed that the wicked are
punished, and the virtuous but unfortunate recompensed, in
the life to come. The parable is, rather, a warning about
God's imminent and this-worldly judgement on the nation of
Israel for its failure to heed God's call to justice and mercy
within its own society, and for its correlated failure to be the
light of the world. It belongs exactly, in other words, with
the other parables of Luke 14—16.

The story is a variation on a folk tale that was well known
in the first-century world – with one dramatic difference. In

the traditional story, the request that somebody be sent back from the dead, to warn people in the present life of what is to come, is normally granted. In this case Jesus declares that his contemporaries knew enough, from their Scriptures, to see that their behaviour was out of line with God's intention, and that even resurrection will not convince them otherwise. At this point, of course, the parable does look ahead to the future life, but it is the future which will, all too soon, break into the present in the resurrection of Jesus himself. Thus the 'rich man' in the parable, like the elder brother in the previous chapter and the steward in the present one, stands for the Israel that is under judgement for its failure to recognize God's moment and fulfil God's call. Like Jeremiah's purchase of a field, even the promise of new life after judgement will not be enough to turn God's people from their present descent into ruin.

The same warning, transposed into a post-Easter key, concludes the first letter to Timothy. The life of the coming age, already given in Jesus and promised to those that are his, contains the true riches; present ones are at best something to be used to God's glory, and at worst 'the root of all evil'. If this is an overstatement, it is not so by much. Faced with the idolatry and greed riches can generate, verse 11 commands us to 'flee all this'; not merely to keep six inches away from it, but to get out and run.

Proper 22

—— ～ ——

Lamentations 1.1–6
2 Timothy 1.1–14
Luke 17.5–10

Paul, in prison, writes about power. Dangerous stuff, we say – tends to corrupt, and all that. Paul's setting, and the work that got him there, guards him from misunderstanding. Tyrants speak of God's power to validate their own; Paul speaks lovingly about God's power to explain why he remains in chains.

God did not give us a spirit of cowardice, he says, but a spirit of power, love and self-control – 1 Corinthians 12, 13 and 14 in a nutshell. Timothy needs reminding that he has a God-given ministry and must not be timid about exercising it. He is not in danger of enjoying God's power too much: rather the reverse. He needs to know that God delights to exercise his power through Christian ministry. But the power of the true God is never mere power; precisely because it is revealed in Jesus Christ, it is always also the power of love, and to be exercised through and in self-control (the word here means 'moderation' or 'prudence' as well as 'self-discipline').

So, Paul continues, in our suffering for the gospel we rely on the power of God. Clearly this is not a power that enables the evangelist to avoid suffering. As he says elsewhere, and as Israel learnt to her cost through the tragic experience of exile, it is a power that is made perfect in our weakness.

When we are at the end of our own resources, then God's power works through us, shedding on the world around that same grace which grasped and saved us. And, finally, God's power will sustain us to the end; when Paul says (v. 12) that God is 'able' to guard until the coming Day that which Paul has entrusted to him (presumably, his whole self), the word he uses is 'powerful'. Unlike the tyrant (in church or home, as well as in nations), Paul's appeal to God's power generates self-giving love and self-forgetful trust.

These are both in evidence in Luke 17. To begin with, one of the great lessons of Christian living: you don't need great faith, you need faith in a great God. The word translated 'mulberry tree' probably referred to the sycamore, which was believed to have especially deep roots; the stress is on the extraordinary power of God when invoked even by apparently tiny faith.

This is followed by the strange saying about worthless slaves. In a culture that all too easily regards God as a faceless and distant dictator, to stress that he doesn't need to thank us for serving him may make the wrong point; it is harder today to get people to see, as Paul says elsewhere (e.g. Colossians 1.10), that God is delighted with our weak efforts. But we certainly need to be reminded, again and again, that nothing we can do can establish a *claim* on God. No amount of prayer, generosity, suffering, organization, teaching, evangelism – nothing puts the God of grace in our debt.

Proper 23

—— ~ ——

Jeremiah 29.1, 4–7
2 *Timothy* 2.8–15
Luke 17.11–19

A sharp-edged summary of Paul's gospel: King Jesus, raised from the dead, of David's seed. The word 'gospel' itself, in Paul's world, meant a royal proclamation; this explains why its heralds fall foul of the authorities. They may be chained, but the gospel itself cannot be; Paul is content with his fate, confident both of the power of the gospel and also of God's future hope for those who endure.

A ministry based on this confidence will not need to descend into disputes about words. This advice could have saved the Church much time, energy and heartache over the last two millennia. Of course, Paul did his own share of arguing; but there is a difference between disputes about words and disputes about the things the words refer to. It takes wisdom to know the difference. The one who does will be the sort of worker who can present the completed project without shame.

Preachers and teachers are sometimes tempted to use this warning about unprofitable word-wrangling as an excuse to serve up a fuzzy generalized message of goodwill, detached from the text. This is either laziness or downright rebellion. The proper alternative to squabbles over words is 'rightly explaining the word of truth'. The verb here is very rare, only occurring otherwise in the Septuagint of Proverbs 3.6

and 11.5, where upright conduct is described in the metaphor of carving out a straight road across difficult terrain. Keeping the metaphor nearly intact here, one might suggest 'leading one's hearers straight to the heart of the text'. To understand the deep meanings of a text, to see where its natural joints and divisions fall, to lay it out so that the hearers may be grasped by its message – that is the vocation that counts.

This task demands hard work. To avoid it becomes a form of ingratitude: for those who live in a world of lies and half-truths, to be entrusted with 'the word of truth' and then to fail to study it and teach it is to be like the nine lepers who, though healed, did not return to give thanks.

The Samaritan who did come back to Jesus was, of course, deeply symbolic for Luke. As elsewhere in his gospel, this is a sign of the breaking down of traditional barriers that kept the Judaean people separate from their northern neighbours, and Jews in general from pagans in general. However, even though it was indeed revolutionary to see the gospel reaching out beyond the borders of the chosen people, it was not alien to Jeremiah's strange message to the exiles. Babylon may have been the great enemy, but now that you are there you must seek its welfare. Paradoxically, the lesson that the exiles had to learn – that God was concerned for the pagan city where they lived – points forward to the explosive gospel message that would one day challenge Jews and pagans alike with the news of another country, another king.

Proper 24

— ❧ —

Jeremiah 31.27–34
2 Timothy 3.14—4.5
Luke 18.1–8

The passages from 2 Timothy and Luke 18 both envisage God's people hanging on, sustaining their energy and sense of direction, even though things seem to go from bad to worse. By contrast, Jeremiah 31 sees through the long night to the new dawn, the new covenant which will replace the broken accord of Sinai. For once, Jeremiah offers the good news that creates hope, giving us light in the darkness, keeping us loyal in prayer (Luke) and teaching (2 Timothy).

Those who remember Jeremiah's original commission in chapters 1 and 2 will hear, as in a great symphony, the early themes returning at last in the major key. Israel, plucked up, broken down, destroyed and overthrown, is now at last to be rebuilt and replanted. Fresh seed will be sown – a new covenant image exploited to the full by Jeremiah's greatest prophetic successor – and God will again woo his bride, will espouse her to himself in an unbreakable bond of love. Those who recognize the same themes in the New Testament – the Church as God's building, God's field, the bride of Christ – will see how thoroughly the early Christians believed that Jeremiah's great words of hope had been fulfilled in Jesus.

Why then do we find ourselves still in the position of the widow coming with dogged persistence before the unjust judge? Of course, as the parable itself makes clear (v. 8a), Jesus is not suggesting that God is like the unjust judge; the argument turns upon the implied contrast as much as upon the semi-parallel. The main thrust is the need for perseverance in prayer.

Jesus' own message looked ahead to the days that would follow his ministry, when his disciples would wait in perplexity through persecution and hardship. The encouragement is equally relevant in our own day, not least for the many Christians under persecution, but not only there. Those who face apathy rather than anger at their Christian witness need just as much to set their faces like a flint, to continue their labour of prayer come what may. And in this work they may find their constant resource in the Scriptures, and in teaching based upon them.

Perhaps not surprisingly, there is little direct teaching in the Bible about the Bible itself. The Bible gets on with being itself, with doing its job rather than with talking about the job it is doing. But precisely at the great moments of transition, one of which is marked by 2 Timothy's reflection of the end of the first Christian generation, it is essential to be reminded of that which will carry God's people through all the changes that come upon them. We who live at a time when sound doctrine is mocked as pompous dogmatism, when teachers of new myths are arising to satisfy those with itching ears, need to return to our roots in order to be reminded of the great theme that tells us who we are 'in the presence of God and of Christ Jesus'.

The Last Sunday After Trinity

—— ⁓ ——

Joel 2.23–end
2 Timothy 4.6–8, 16–18
Luke 18.9–14

The harvest and the law court are the lenses through which the prophet gazes, wide-eyed, into God's future. Rain in abundance – easy to forget, in northern Europe, what a relief that would be in the Middle East – and the barns and vats will be overflowing. The sinister, almost surrealist, army of locusts which had ravaged Israel at the command of her God in the previous chapters has gone. The years that the locust had eaten will be restored to them, in a promise destined to become proverbial in its own right.

Feasting and thanksgiving will mean more than merely living happily ever after. The harvest will be literal, but will also point to the restored relationship between YHWH and his people. It will mean the people's *vindication* (v. 23); it happens in order that 'my people shall never again be put to shame' (v. 26, repeated in the following verse). In a culture where honour and shame were everything, Israel had been ashamed because the harvest had failed, hanging her head before the watching world. That, paradoxically, is the clue. Pride and wilful self-sufficiency had brought the locusts, with YHWH himself at their head (2.11); now the humble will be exalted, vindicated in the divine lawcourt. 'It was this man, not the other one, who went down to his house justified' – the one mention of 'justification' on the lips of Jesus.

People often balk at lawcourt imagery in theology, supposing it to leave us with a picture of God as a cold or legalistic judge. The language belongs, of course, in a world where true justice was as welcome (and at least as rare) as the rain needed for good harvests; where society trembled on the brink of either chaos or tyranny; and where stories of a Solomon, dispensing God's justice with clarity and wisdom, were like golden fairy tales to which the regular response would be 'If only!'. We who take justice for granted (at least, until you take part in a lawsuit yourself) can ill afford to ignore its near absence, or grievous distortions, in much of the world, both on a large and a small scale – and its constant occurrence as scriptural theme, not least in Jesus and Paul.

One of the theological tasks of our day is to learn how to tell the parable of the two men in the Temple so that it shocks and surprises our world as Jesus' story did his, opening up a vision of God's justice which is not fooled by possessions and prestige, or by social standing, but sees to the heart, and hears the genuine cry of the penitent sinner. Or, to put it another way, we need to discover how Paul's famous doctrine of 'justification', which in Romans is part of the revelation of 'God's justice', is part of, perhaps even a pointer towards, the justice that will be done by 'the Lord, the righteous judge', of whom the same Paul speaks in today's epistle.

Sundays Before Advent

The Fourth Sunday Before Advent

———— ≈ ————

Isaiah 1.10–18
2 Thessalonians 1.1–12
Luke 19.1–10

Luke cuts Zacchaeus even more down to size, describing him with affected pomposity ('he was a chief tax-collector! He was rich!') and then pointing out that he was also a bit too small for his own good. Luke here highlights several themes which sum up what Jesus' ministry has been all about and point to the reasons for the forthcoming events.

Zacchaeus stands for the ambiguity of the Judaism of Jesus' day. Compromised with Rome, yet conscious of status; aware of a need for renewal, yet clinging to ways of living which made that renewal impossible; children of Abraham, yet lost. Jesus' response, as ever, is to come shamelessly to where the pain is: 'he has gone in to eat with a man who is a sinner' (v. 7) looks back to the accusation in 15.2, and on to the mocking on the cross, when Jesus was for the last time 'numbered with the transgressors' (22.37).

This sharing and bearing of the sinner's blame is undertaken out of a sovereign vocation. 'The Son of Man came to seek and save the lost'; and here he is, accepting Zacchaeus's confession and promise of restitution, assuring not only him but the suspicious onlookers that Zacchaeus is now a saved child of Abraham. In other words, Jesus is acting, and Zacchaeus is treating him, as if he were a priest, or, more, as if he were the Temple itself. We should not, then, be surprised at how the chapter develops. When Jesus comes to Jerusalem, the place simply isn't big enough for him and the Temple side by side. He has staked a claim, that what the Temple stood for is now fulfilled in him. Zacchaeus has staked his own life upon that claim, and Luke invites all his readers to do the same. But to understand why salvation came to the tax-collector's house, and why it comes to ours, we need to read on, to allow Luke's final chapters to unveil the mystery which characters in his story could only glimpse.

The almost comic tone of the story, and its happy ending, cannot disguise the seriousness of the issues. Isaiah addressed Israel at a time when rebellion against YHWH was so rife that, instead of speaking to 'Israel' or 'Jacob', the words that came most naturally were 'Sodom' and 'Gomorrah', bywords for wickedness and consequent judgement. In that state, the practice of religion is worse than useless, an attempt to draw the veil of respectable practice over mouldering injustices. The only thing that matters is what Zacchaeus discovered: repentance and restoration.

Paul, standing in the same prophetic tradition but the further side of the gospel events, surveys the whole world with essentially the same message. We recoil from warnings of judgement, knowing how easily such language is abused. But judgement is the necessary obverse of justice; and if God is not interested in justice, not only Isaiah and Luke, but also Jesus himself, were all deeply mistaken.

The Third Sunday
Before Advent

—— ∼ ——

Job 19.23–27a
2 Thessalonians 2.1–5, 13–17
Luke 20.27–38

The overall theme ('resurrection') is obvious, but the detail is daunting.

It seems a shame, as the translators' footnotes say, that the Hebrew of Job 19.26 is 'incomprehensible'. The old version ('and though worms destroy this body, yet in my flesh shall I see God') is engraved on innumerable minds and hearts, courtesy of George Frederick Handel. But, though the passage doesn't predict the Christian doctrine of resurrection quite as the older translators supposed, the modified account is in some ways more moving. Job, at the end of his tether, affirms that justice will be done; that a defending counsel will live and arise (the word, in the Hebrew and the Septuagint, would have suggested 'resurrection' to readers of Jesus' day) to plead his cause; and that God himself, who for so long had seemed to be his adversary, would be on his side at the last. Take Job as an icon of the whole world, groaning in travail, longing for justice and new life, and you can translate his confidence directly into the cosmic hope of Romans 8.

And then there is 2 Thessalonians 2, with omissions that leave the 'mystery of lawlessness' and the 'restrainer' in interpretative limbo for yet another year. What we are left with is enough to be going on with: a legacy of naive literalism means that at any mention of the 'second coming' we think of clouds, raptures, and Jesus flying around like a self-propelled spaceman. Paul clearly can't be talking about such an event, since in verse 2 he warns the Thessalonians not to be alarmed at getting a letter telling them that the Day of the Lord has arrived. If this referred to a 'cosmic meltdown' one would suppose that the Thessalonians would have noticed. The truth seems more mysterious: through this-worldly events (as we would call them), God will defeat the mysterious cunning of evil, and rescue his people at last. The note of confidence in the face of superhuman adversity is what matters at the end.

And so to the Sadducees' question, and Jesus' answer – which apparently satisfied, even stunned, his hearers, but which leaves us bewildered. Surely the point Jesus was supposed to prove was not *survival* (Abraham, Isaac and Jacob are still alive somewhere), but *resurrection* (they will rise again to new bodily life)? Yes; but often enough, in rabbinic-style arguments, the game of chess is called off two or three moves early, once both parties can see how the land lies. For most Jews, with their strong theology of the goodness of the created physical world, disembodied existence could never be a final desired resting place. As long as Jesus could show that the patriarchs were still alive in God's presence, the final move ('they will therefore rise again') could be left unstated. Our apologetic, not least to worried souls within our own flocks, needs to be as shrewd, and as sharply attuned to the assumptions and questions of our time.

The Second Sunday
Before Advent

—— ⁓ ——

Malachi 4.1–2a
2 Thessalonians 3.6–13
Luke 21.5–19

Warnings against idleness seem irrelevant in our culture. Those who have work seem to have more and more of it; those who don't seem stuck in a trap. No doubt there are shades of grey, and some manage to play the system; but few today are idle by choice.

Paul's warnings, though, shed an interesting light on his teaching. The idleness against which he warns wasn't caused by his eschatological preaching (the world's going to end, so why work?). It was the result of his teaching that Christians should live as brothers and sisters in a world where siblings formed a single socio-economic unit. Part of the meaning of *agape* was the very practical (and politically subversive) one of mutual support. Now he addresses the flip side of the coin: each must contribute to the best of their ability, not simply sponge off the others. It is ironic that today these warnings might apply to welfare scroungers rather than to anything that goes on within the Church.

There is plenty of eschatological warning in the other two readings. As usual, though, we have to be careful before jumping to the wrong conclusion. Luke's Olivet discourse is emphatically and specifically about the fall of Jerusalem, not about the end of the world. As such, it may of course be taken as a model for all living that peers into an uncertain future, needing to trust in God when everything is crashing down around one's ears. The Church in many parts of the world lives with wars, rumours of wars, purges and persecutions on a daily basis; those of us who don't should read passages like this in prayerful family solidarity with those who do. A church not being persecuted should also, sometimes, ask itself why not. Martyrs and confessors around today's world will testify to us, never mind to their oppressors, that God is faithful to his promises, providing words, wisdom and above all perseverance.

And, of course, the hope of justice. The little passage from Malachi (why not read the whole chapter? It's only six verses!) may make some shudder with distaste, but the news that the God who made and loves the world will at the last put all wrongs to right is great and good news, to be clung to precisely in a world where everything seems upside down and inside out. The same sun that rises to scorch the plants that have gone to the bad is the sun that brings healing in its wings for 'you who revere my name'. This is because, of course, it is the 'sun of righteousness', or the 'sun of justice' (how often Bible translators need an English word that holds both of those together the way the Hebrew and Greek do). God's utter loyalty to his creation means that he will put everything right at the last, and when his human creatures trust his loyalty they will in turn be assured that justice will bring healing, not destruction.

Christle the King

— ~ —

Jeremiah 23.1–6
Colossians 1.11–20
Luke 23.33–43

Shepherds, shepherding stories, and shepherding metaphors abound throughout the Bible, as one would expect in that culture. The creative thing in Israel's traditions, though, was the development of 'the shepherd' as a metaphor first for the king (the lowly status of shepherds makes this daring), and then for God himself. These traditions explode like fireworks in the Gospels as Jesus, who probably never herded a sheep in his life, reuses them to explain his strange activity.

Jeremiah's polemic against the wicked shepherds goes with the preceding denunciation of the rump of the Davidic house. Hezekiah and Josiah have not been able to save Judah from the slide into shame, exile and devastation; the would-be shepherds, Jehoiachin and his like, have done nothing to look after God's sheep. In that setting, God promises to gather his sheep once more, and to set wise and caring shepherds over them.

Rising out of this promise, but far transcending it, is the pledge that God will raise up a 'branch of righteousness' who will put God's justice into effect, who will create salvation for God's people. This Davidic king will bear a strange name: 'Yahweh is our righteousness'. He will embody God's own promise, covenant faithfulness, justice and loyalty.

What will this look like in practice? Imagine Luke

126

answering this question by tearing down a curtain in front of a great but deeply shocking painting. Here is the king who embodies the justice, the loyalty, the salvation of God: praying for those who nail him to the cross, mocked as a false king, taunted as Jeremiah taunted Jehoiachin as though he were a mere sham, an impostor. Here he is, fulfilling God's promise to bring in his kingdom of justice and mercy, rescuing those who turn to him and his kingdom only when all other hope is exhausted. Is this, or is this not, asks Luke, what Jeremiah (and so many others) was talking about? Is this not the shepherd who would embody the saving faithfulness of God?

Colossians 1.15–20, in effect, sets all this to music. The grand poem, in which verses 15–16 balance 18b–20, with 17 and 18a themselves balanced in the middle, exploits some of the most deep-rooted Jewish language about God – that of the 'wisdom' through which God made all things – in order to talk about Jesus. He is the one through whom all things were made – and redeemed; he is the one who now embodies the ruling and reconciling work of the creator God, Israel's God. What seems bold and daring, almost oxymoronic, when we meet it in Jeremiah, is woven so closely together here as to seem almost natural. Why should not the living God come to live among us as a creature bearing God's image? Why should he not be the first-born from the dead? And why (we ask with fear and trembling) should he not unveil his royal splendour most fully when engaged in the bloody work of peacemaking?

The Society for Promoting Christian Knowledge (SPCK) was founded in 1698. Its mission statement is:

To promote Christian knowledge by
- **Communicating the Christian faith in its rich diversity**
- **Helping people to understand the Christian faith and to develop their personal faith; and**
- **Equipping Christians for mission and ministry**

SPCK Worldwide serves the Church through Christian literature and communication projects in 100 countries, and provides books for those training for ministry in many parts of the developing world. This worldwide service depends upon the generosity of others and all gifts are spent wholly on ministry programmes, without deductions.

SPCK Bookshops support the life of the Christian community by making available a full range of Christian literature and other resources, providing support for those training for ministry, and assisting bookstalls and book agents throughout the UK.

SPCK Publishing produces Christian books and resources, covering a wide range of inspirational, pastoral, practical and academic subjects. Authors are drawn from many different Christian traditions, and publications aim to meet the needs of a wide variety of readers in the UK and throughout the world.

The Society does not necessarily endorse the individual views contained in its publications, but hopes they stimulate readers to think about and further develop their Christian faith.

For information about the Society, visit our website at *www.spck.org.uk*, or write to:
SPCK, Holy Trinity Church, Marylebone Road, London NW1 4DU, United Kingdom.